First Edition

triumphlearning™

Common Core Coach

English Language Arts 5

Common Core Coach, English Language Arts, First Edition, Grade 5   T104NA   ISBN-13: 978-1-61997-432-6
Cover Design: Q2A/Bill Smith   **Cover Illustration:** Elizabeth Rosen

Contents

W.5.2.a–e; W.5.4; W.5.5;
W.5.6; W.5.7; W.5.8; W.5.9.b;
W.5.10; SL.5.1; L.5.3.a; L.5.4.c

RI.5.1; RI.5.4; RI.5.5; RI.5.7;
RI.5.10; RF.5.4.a; SL.5.1

W.5.3.a–e; W.5.4; W.5.5;
W.5.6; W.5.8; W.5.10; SL.5.1;
L.5.1.b–d; L.5.2.b, c; L.5.4.a;
L.5.5.c

RL.5.1; RL.5.2; RL.5.3; RL.5.4;
RL.5.5; RL.5.10; RF.5.4.a;
SL.5.1

Reading Short Stories

Look at this underwater scene. Do you think this would be a good setting for a story? Why or why not?

ESSENTIAL QUESTION

What are the important parts of a good short story?

Consider ▶ How do you get to know the characters in a short story?

Can you usually tell right away whether you like the characters?

A Snare for Srayosi

Chapter 1

1   Srayosi tried to wriggle free from the ropes around her wrists and ankles and then looked over at her twin brother. Shah was gesturing desperately, shaking his head back and forth wildly. Like Srayosi, his hands and feet were tied, and they were both trapped underwater, at the bottom of an aquarium tank designed for marine mammals, not humans.

Srayosi knew that average people can hold their breath for approximately thirty seconds. Luckily, Srayosi and Shah were far from average. They would have exactly seven minutes and twelve seconds to escape from their bindings and swim to the surface. The twin teens had been practicing holding their breath since they were babies. It was part of how they grew up.

SHORT STORY A short story is a short fictional narrative with a beginning, middle, and ending. A short story is told in far fewer words than a novel. Important parts of a short story are characters, setting, and plot. What characters are described on this page? What do you learn about them?

NARRATOR The narrator of a short story is the person who tells the story. If the story is told by one of the characters in the story, it is told from the first-person point of view. In first-person point of view, the narrator uses the pronoun *I*. If the story is told by someone who is not a character in the story, it is told from the third-person point of view. In third-person point of view, the narrator uses the pronouns *he*, *she*, and *they*. Who is the narrator of this story? How do you know?

Unluckily, their focus on escaping was interrupted by a loud grinding noise. The walls of the tank began to move inward, making the room inside the tank smaller and smaller, while the water rose higher and higher. Srayosi and Shah might have six minutes of breath left, but they would be crushed in less than three.

Srayosi's mind began racing faster and faster. She calculated that she had forty-five seconds to think of a solution and two minutes to get untied, untie Shah, swim to the top of the tank, and climb out. Fifteen seconds had already ticked away.

5   Srayosi looked for a tool she could use to get the ropes off her hands. But then Srayosi noticed that the glass floor of the tank was covered with slimy algae. She scooped some of it into her fingers and began to rub it on the ropes around her wrists.

Srayosi wriggled her wrists back and forth and scrunched her long, narrow fingers as tightly as possible. The slippery algae helped reduce the friction between her skin and the rope. In less than twenty seconds, Srayosi's hands were free.

PLOT The plot of a story is its series of events. The first part of the plot tells the story's basic situation—the characters, setting, and conflict. The conflict is a problem or struggle that the characters must face. As the characters deal with the problem, obstacles get in their way. The problem or conflict grows more and more serious; we describe this by saying that the action "rises." The point where the problem is most serious is called the climax, or the high point, of the story. What problems have Srayosi and Shah faced so far?

If Shah could have spoken, he would have said, "Great, Sis!" Instead, he followed her lead and began scooping up algae, too. There was just one problem. Srayosi and Shah were twins, but physically, they couldn't have been more different. Srayosi was small and thin, while Shah was tall and muscular. Shah's size usually came in handy, but his huge size wasn't very useful at the moment.

Most people saw Shah's size and made the assumption that he was a hothead. In reality, Shah was able to remain cool in even the most torturous circumstances. In this situation, Shah quickly understood that no matter how much algae he used, he was never going to wriggle his humongous hands through the ropes. He began to meditate, knowing that his sister would figure a way out for the both of them. She always did.

Chapter 2

Exactly one and a half minutes had passed, and Srayosi was completely untied. She knew that she didn't have time to untie Shah completely. She also knew that she couldn't leave him there. Srayosi had only one firm plan in mind. She would untie the weight that was holding Shah down, push him to the surface, climb out of the tank, and then pull her brother to safety.

10   Step one was a bit challenging. Srayosi had no prior experience with the knot connecting the rope to the weight. But her quick wit and able fingers worked in harmony, and she untied Shah in twenty-seven seconds. The next step was not very challenging at all. Srayosi gave Shah a shove, and he wiggled his way to the surface of the water. Shah even gave Srayosi a nod as he swam to the surface. This was going better than Srayosi had imagined.

She climbed up onto the surface of the tank and grabbed Shah under his arms. Then she pulled with all her might. Nothing happened. She couldn't lift Shah's massive, wet body out of the tank.

NARRATOR A narrator can have different points of view. If the point of view is omniscient, the narrator knows the thoughts and feelings of all the characters in the story. If the point of view is limited, the narrator knows only one character's thoughts and feelings.

Sometimes a narrator expresses an opinion by the way he or she tells a story. Other times, the narrator is objective. The narrator presents the action and the characters' speech without comment or emotion and does not reveal the thoughts of the characters. The reader has to interpret them and uncover their meaning. How does the narrator's point of view in this story influence how events are described?

The tank's walls were now about four feet apart. Shah was at least three feet wide himself. Srayosi felt defeated, but she wasn't about to give up. That's when she heard the sound of footsteps.

"The IOATP!" Srayosi yelled. "They're coming, Shah! You've got to get out. DO SOMETHING!"

As it turned out, Srayosi was the hothead. She had tried meditating, but it was never her thing. When the going got tough, Srayosi's blood started boiling. She believed this made her brain work fast when she was under pressure. But now, she was at her wit's end. They had to get out before the IOATP found them.

15   The IOATP were the International Organization Against Teen Power. Srayosi and Shah were part of an international society of teens trained since birth to fight crime and injustice. They weren't superheroes, but they were pretty super. Villains everywhere hated them and formed their own group to battle them—the IOATP. They had put Srayosi and Shah in the tank in the first place.

Srayosi tried one last time to lift her brother from the tank. The footsteps were right behind her. Things were bad, yet Shah was smiling.

"Mom!" Shah cheered as his muscled mother reached past Srayosi and pulled him to safety. Srayosi had inherited her mother's hotheadedness, but it was Shah who got her size and strength.

"How did you find us?" Srayosi wondered aloud.

"Shah and I have been working on meditative transmissions," she explained. "He's able to send me mental pictures when he meditates. I saw where you were, and I knew you needed me."

20 "Mom to the rescue," Shah said.

"Always!" their mom replied lovingly. "Now let's get out of here. I set some explosives, and they're about to go off in 5 . . . 4 . . . 3 . . . 2 . . ."

PLOT The plot of a story ends when the problems have been resolved. This is called the resolution. What is the resolution of this story?

THEME The theme of a short story is its message about life. Usually, the author doesn't directly tell you the theme. You have to figure it out yourself by looking at the characters, their words and actions, and the setting of the story. What do you think is the theme of this story?

Comprehension Check

Think about what you learned about the main characters in "A Snare for Srayosi."
Look back through the story for evidence that tells you about their character
traits in the things they do, the words they say, and in how they are described.
Think about how they are alike and how they are different. Then use the
information to fill in the Venn diagram below.

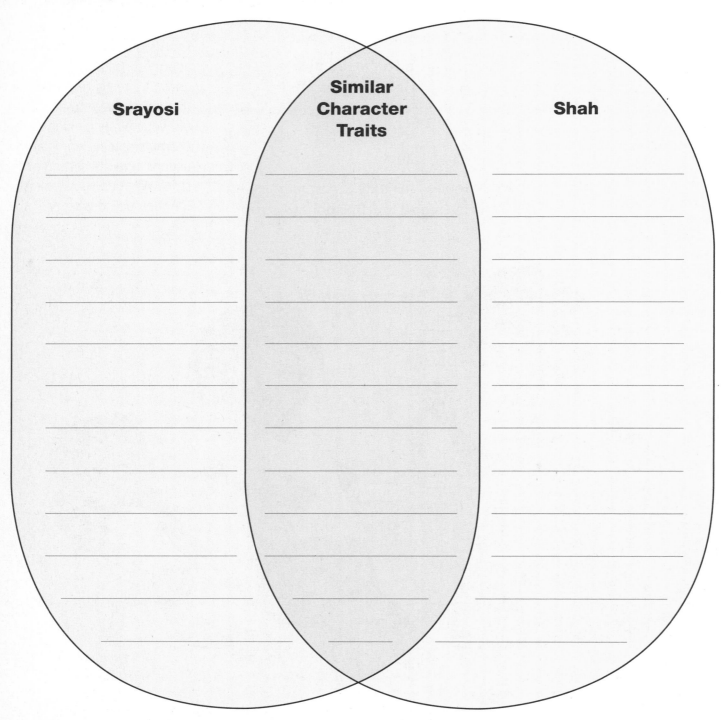

Srayosi

Similar Character Traits

Shah

Vocabulary

Use the word map below to help you define and use one of the highlighted vocabulary words from the Share and Learn selection you are about to read or another word you choose.

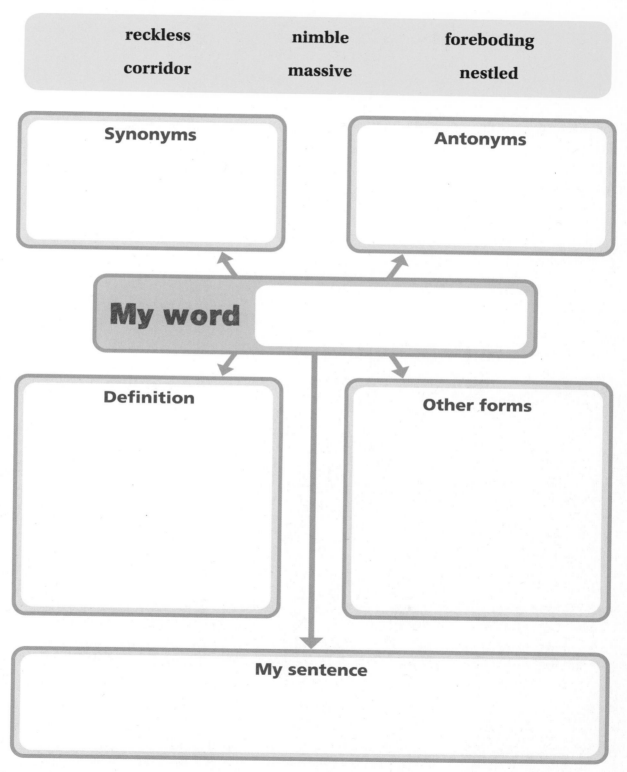

reckless   nimble   foreboding

corridor   massive   nestled

Synonyms

Antonyms

My word

Definition

Other forms

My sentence

Consider ▶ How do you feel when you go to a place you've never been before?

Do you like to rush right in or take your time?

Into the Maze

CHARACTER TRAITS

What do you learn about the traits of Theo and his friend Ariana early in the story?

_____

_____

Underline the words that tell you about Theo, and circle the words that describe Ariana.

1   Theo took one tentative step into the corn maze, then stopped in his tracks. He grabbed a dried husk and examined it. The corn stalk had to be at least double his height, around twelve feet tall. The plants were packed together so tightly, it was difficult to see through them. Walls of corn wound this way and that, with no end in sight. For a place that was supposed to be the area's main attraction, it was eerily quiet. Of course, Ariana had raced right in. "Act first, think later" was her motto.

"Ariana!" Theo shout-whispered to his best friend. "Come back!"

Ariana rushed back to the start of the maze, breathless. Her cheeks were flushed with excitement.

"This is so cool, Theo!" she said. "What are you waiting for?"

5 "I'm waiting because it's the right thing to do, Ariana," Theo said sensibly. "We can't just rush in here without having a plan."

"Oh, right, a plan," Ariana replied. "You're the planner. What's our plan?"

Theo sighed. He loved Ariana's sense of adventure. She was willing to do anything and go anywhere on a moment's notice, like heading to this strange place just because their new team trainer had given her a "special event" pass to it.

Mr. Minos was okay as far as trainers go, but Theo wasn't about to follow him to the ends of the earth—or into a deserted maze, especially when they had the big lacrosse championship game later that day. Seriously, Ariana should have known better. But she had been too excited about the adventure to worry about the game.

"Ariana, I agree that this looks like an interesting place," Theo said. "But why isn't anybody here? Isn't this supposed to be a special event?"

10 "It is a little odd, Theo," Ariana said. "But you're the one who made us leave the dorms an hour before we needed to. Maybe everyone's coming fashionably late."

"Doubtful," Theo said. "Anyway, I'm not taking another step into this maze until we figure out a way to track our path. If we can find the way we went in, we can always find a way out."

"Good plan, planner," Ariana replied as she shuffled through the pockets of her windbreaker. "Except that I didn't bring anything we could use. I only have a blue highlighter I forgot to take out of my pocket the last time I wore this jacket."

"That will do," Theo said. "We can mark a stalk every few feet."

MAKE CONNECTIONS BETWEEN TEXTS How are Theo and Ariana similar to the twins Srayosi and Shah in the previous story? How are they different?

_____

_____

_____

NARRATOR Who is telling this story? Is the story told from a limited or omniscient point of view? Is the narrator objective? How do you know?

_____

_____

_____

PLOT What is the conflict in this story?

_____

_____

How can you tell the action of the story is rising, or that the conflict is growing more serious?

_____

_____

Underline the sentence that shows rising action.

MAKE CONNECTIONS: TEXT-TO-SELF Have you ever traveled to an unfamiliar place with a friend or relative? How did having someone to share the adventure with affect your experience?

_____

_____

_____

The two friends headed into the maze. The fall air was crisp and brisk, and now that he had a plan in place, Theo decided to relax and enjoy the experience. He liked spending time with Ariana, even though she could be a little reckless at times. Plus, it was a good opportunity to go over their game plan. Since Theo was the goalie and Ariana a defender, they needed to work together and communicate well. Ariana had a lot more experience than he did. While they talked about game strategy, Theo's shoulders began to drop and his forehead unfurrowed. And that's when the giant metal crow swooped down from the sky.

15 "DUCK!" a voice boomed as loud as thunder.

Theo and Ariana used their nimble, athletic reflexes to duck to the ground just before the robot bird reached them.

"What is that?" Theo yelled to Ariana. "And who told us to duck?"

"RUN!" the invisible voice commanded.

"I don't know!" Ariana screamed back. "But I think we'd better listen!"

20 Theo led the dash down the path. The mechanical flying beast turned awkwardly above the maze and headed back toward them.

"STOP!" the voice roared.

"Stop?" Ariana questioned. "That doesn't seem like such great advice."

Theo had already stopped in his tracks.

"Whoever it is, I think we'd better pay attention," Theo said. "Look!"

25 Theo pointed to a hoe that was lying on the ground. Ariana picked it up and smiled. The best defense is a good offense.

Ariana looked up as the creature came closer and closer toward them. She could see a space in the joint that held the wing to the bird's body. She had one chance, so her aim would have to be perfect. The crow dove toward them, and Ariana raised the stick side of the hoe and lodged it in the joint. The gears inside the crow started grinding. The crow tumbled and then crashed to the ground, its gears clanging loudly for a moment until they stopped working completely.

"Okay, you were right," Ariana said to Theo. "This place is creepy. We should just get back to the dorms."

"Great plan," Theo agreed. "But we didn't have time to mark our path when we were running away from the crow. So . . . which way do we go?"

"We came this way," Ariana said as she led Theo back down the path. "And then we turned right, and then left, and then, well, then I'm not so sure, honestly."

30   "Me neither," Theo admitted. "I think we made another left."

"ARE YOU SURE?" the voice boomed. "YOU SHOULD BE SURE."

CITE EVIDENCE Why was Ariana reminded that "looks are often deceiving"?

_____

_____

Underline the sentences that explain your answer.

MAKE CONNECTIONS BETWEEN TEXTS How is the plot of this story similar to the plot of "A Snare for Srayosi"? How are the plots different?

_____

_____

_____

"Who are you?" Theo yelled back. "And if you want to help us, just tell us how to get out of here."

"BWAHAHAHA!" the foreboding voice laughed. "I COULD, BUT I WON'T. YOU'RE BOTH SCHOLAR-ATHLETES. YOU SHOULD BE ABLE TO FIGURE IT OUT FOR YOURSELVES."

"Gee, thanks for the compliment," Ariana replied. "Much appreciated."

35 "DON'T MOCK THE MAZE MASTER," the voice warned. "YOU WILL REGRET IT."

"Sorry," Ariana answered. "Didn't know you were so touchy."

"Let's just go," Theo said. "I'm pretty sure it was left."

Ariana followed Theo as he led her through the winding maze. He turned the corner quickly and headed down a long corridor of corn, then turned right at the end of the path, then made another quick left. He definitely looked as if he knew where he was going. But when they came to a dead end at a solid wall of corn, Ariana was reminded that looks are often deceiving.

"I'm sorry, Ari," Theo apologized. "I really thought we went left."

40   "No problem, Theo," Ariana replied. "I got us into this mess. I'll get us out."

Ariana started back the way they had come. The sun was rising higher in the sky as the day got closer to noon. Even though the autumn weather was cool, Ariana took off her jacket and tied it around her waist. All the running and worrying was making her hot.

"PUT YOUR JACKET BACK ON!" the voice ordered. "YOU'RE GOING TO NEED A WINDBREAKER."

"Um . . . okay," Ariana said. "What does that mean?"

Ariana and Theo turned as they heard an unfamiliar sound in the distance. The sound swirled and whirled, and when the two turned the next corner of the maze, they saw an immense vortex headed their way.

45   "TORNADO TIME!" the Maze Master informed them. "ARE YOU READY FOR A WEATHER EMERGENCY?"

This time it was Ariana who shouted the commands.

"RUN!" she yelled as she grabbed Theo's hand and led him away from the tornado.

"PULL!" she cried as she grabbed a corn stalk and ripped it from the ground.

"DIG!" she commanded as she scooped away dirt to make a trench in the ground.

AUTHOR'S BACKGROUND AND CULTURE The author lives in a large city but spends her summers in the country, where there are corn mazes. How might this story be different if the author had never seen a corn maze?

_____

_____

_____

MAKE CONNECTIONS BETWEEN TEXTS Both this story and "A Snare for Srayosi" include mysterious or unexplained elements. What are the most mysterious elements of each story?

_____

_____

_____

PLOT Ariana and Theo survive the tornado. Do you think this is where the conflict will end? Why or why not?

50 Ariana and Theo jumped into the trench and lay flat in it. Ariana pulled the corn stalks over them. They held hands and waited. And waited. The tornado never came. It must have headed down another corn aisle before it disappeared. Ariana and Theo emerged from the trench.

"Hey, Ari, that was impressively quick thinking," Theo said. "But did you really think a little trench and some dead corn stalks were going to protect us from a tornado?"

Ariana playfully punched her friend and laughed out loud.

"Well, it was better than nothing!" she replied.

Theo brushed the husks from his clothing, then off of Ariana's back.

55 "Wow, look at that!" he said as he pointed in the distance.

The tornado hadn't hit them, but it had damaged the maze. There was a large, clear circle where fields of corn had been standing only a few minutes earlier.

"I bet if we search the edges of that circle, we'll find one of our highlights!" Ariana said.

"Great minds think alike!" Theo replied. "That's just what I was thinking. You go left, and I'll go right. We'll meet at the bottom of the circle. This way we can do the search in half the time."

"Great plan, as always," said Ariana. "Let's go!"

60   Ariana knew that they had made the highlights at eye level, so she quickly started around the circle, looking for a sign that they had been down a path before. She was nearly at the bottom of the circle when she saw the blue highlight on the brown, dried leaf.

    "Theo!" she yelled. "I found it!"

    But when Ariana turned around, Theo was nowhere in sight. And that's when she heard him scream.

    Ariana raced toward the sound of Theo's voice. She darted down a row of corn and almost raced into the most massive spider web she had ever seen in her life. Then she stepped back and gasped. Theo was trapped by the web. And a giant spider was headed his way!

    "YOU NEED TO TAKE CONTROL, ARIANA," the voice directed.

65   "Control? What's that supposed to mean?" Ariana asked. "And how do you know my name?"

    Ariana spied something small and black nestled in the light brown leaves. It was a remote control. The spider was two long-legged steps away from her teammate. Theo had stopped screaming and had closed his eyes. Ariana did need to take control. She pushed the stop button, and the spider became immobile.

MAKE CONNECTIONS: TEXT-TO-WORLD How are the events in this story like events that could happen in the real world? How are they unlike real-world events?

_____

_____

_____

PLOT The climax is the high point in the action of a short story. What is the climax of this story?

_____

_____

Underline the sentences that tell you about it.

SEQUENCE OF EVENTS
Underline the sentence that tells about events that happened prior to the events described in the story.

PLOT What is the resolution of this story?

_____

_____

_____

DETERMINE THEME
What do you think the theme of this story is? How is it similar to the theme of the story "A Snare for Srayosi"? How is it different?

_____

_____

_____

_____

Ariana pulled Theo from the web. They rushed back to the entrance of the maze just as sirens began to blare. Two police cruisers pulled up, and the team's lacrosse coach, Ms. Ethra, jumped out of one of them.

"Where's Mr. Minos?" she questioned.

"Mr. Minos?" asked Ariana. "What's he got to do with this?"

70 "YOU'LL NEVER FIND ME!" the voice challenged.

"Mr. Minos!" Theo and Ariana said at the same time.

"When your teammates told me Mr. Minos had given you the pass to the maze, I started wondering," Ms. Ethra explained.

"Mr. Minos holds the state record for saves," a police officer explained. "He was a goalie twenty years ago, and no one's even come close since then. But he knew that the combination of a hot goalie with a stellar defender was a real threat. He decided to eliminate the competition."

"I NEVER MEANT TO HURT YOU," Mr. Minos called through the air. "I JUST WANTED YOU TO MISS THE GAME."

75 "We'll take care of him," the officer assured them. "But you two have a game to play. You'd better go."

Theo and Ariana got in the car and smiled at each other. They'd have just enough time on the ride back to finalize their game plan. It was going to be the best one ever.

Anchor Standard Discussion Questions

Discuss the following questions with your peer group. Then record your answers in the space provided.

1. Do you think Theo and Ariana are ever in real danger in the story? Why or why not? Support your answer with details from the text.

_____

_____

_____

_____

_____

_____

2. Look back at the words the narrator uses to describe Theo and Ariana throughout the story. Do you think the narrator favors one character over the other? Explain why or why not, citing specific details from the text as support.

_____

_____

_____

_____

_____

_____

Comprehension Check

1. Why do Theo and Ariana go to the corn maze?

_____

_____

_____

2. Do you think Theo and Ariana work well together as a team? Cite details from the text that support your opinion.

_____

_____

_____

3. Based on what you know about Theo and Ariana, do you think they will win the lacrosse championship? Why or why not?

_____

_____

_____

Read On Your Own

Read another story, "The Famous Merkel," independently. Apply what you learned in this lesson and check your understanding.

Reading Drama

What do you see these characters doing in this photograph? What do you think is happening in the play they are performing?

ESSENTIAL QUESTION

How is a play a special way of telling a story?

Consider ▶ What special qualities does a student need to become class president?

How can a student demonstrate those qualities?

Stage Fright

Cast of Characters:

Chris, a candidate for class president

Terry, a campaign manager

Robin, a campaign manager

Scene 1

In a schoolroom, Terry and Robin sit on folding chairs, facing a podium. Between the chairs and podium there is a third chair for Chris. Chris enters but doesn't sit in the chair. He stands restlessly and sometimes paces back and forth.

DRAMA: SCENES A drama, or play, is often divided into parts or sections called scenes. The first scene usually sets up the situation and introduces a conflict or problem. What problem does Chris have in this scene?

1 **Chris:** Hi, Terry. Hi, Robin.

Robin: Hi, Chris. Did you finish writing your speech?

Chris: *(Chris looks concerned and waves a paper in the air.)* I wrote it last night . . . but I wish it were better.

Terry: Did you use the notes we made?

5 **Chris:** I started to, but then Monica called to tell me I shouldn't run against her, and while I was on the phone, my little sister spilled spaghetti sauce on the paper, and then I couldn't read what the notes said. *(Chris shakes his head, discouraged.)*

MAKE INFERENCES Sometimes you must use details from a selection and what you already know to figure out something that is not stated directly. This is called making an inference. The author does not directly state that Chris is nervous about making a speech. What details in the play help you infer that he is nervous about the speech?

Robin: Are you okay?

Chris: I wish there were a way to get elected without giving a speech.

Terry: I don't think there is. Both candidates for class president are required to give a speech.

Robin: My dad says making a speech is always hard, and he does a lot of speaking.

10   **Chris:** I think your dad is right.

Terry: Chris, everybody has to do it, and it's just as hard for them as it is for you. Just try it at the podium.

Chris: You think I should stand at the podium?

Robin: Think of the podium as your friend. You can rest your written speech on it, in case you need to look at it. You can even hang on to it if you're feeling fidgety—just rest your hands on the sides.

Terry: Don't hide behind it, that's all.

15   **Chris:** I'll try it without the podium. *(He begins his speech, rocking back and forth from one foot to the other.)* 'Ladies and gentlemen. I'm Chris for president. Uh—we are all students.' *(He starts to slowly wander.)* 'But we are people first.' *(He stops wandering, starts to tremble, and then to shake. He struggles to hold the paper still.)* 'Also . . . I'm also a student . . . and also a person,' *(He wipes his brow twice.)* 'like anybody else!' *(He stops the speech, breathing heavily.)*

SEQUENCE OF EVENTS
The scenes in a drama involve a sequence of events, or a series of things that happen. How does the sequence of events in this scene develop tension in the play?

Terry: Are you that nervous reading aloud in class?

Chris: No. That's not nearly as bad.

Robin: Have you ever acted in a play?

Chris: A long time ago, but that was different . . .

20 **Terry:** If you've done those things, you can give a speech, no problem. Do you talk about your platform in your speech?

Chris: What platform? We give the speeches on the auditorium stage.

Terry: Not that kind of platform!

Chris: You mean, do I talk about my position on important issues?

Robin: Exactly. You have to tell people what you believe in and what you think should be done. Monica thinks we should all wear uniforms at school. Monica's platform in the election is that students should be able to vote *for* or *against* school uniforms. She says if kids are all dressed the same way, they won't make fun of each other.

25 **Chris:** Uniforms won't solve the teasing problem. What will help is caring about each other. If we all learn to appreciate each other, people won't get teased.

Robin: Maybe uniforms would help some, but I don't want to wear a uniform. And Chantal told me that the reason Monica had that idea was because she gets teased about her clothes by two of the other girls.

Terry: *(To Chris.)* Okay, so school uniforms are not part of your platform.

Robin: I think the question is, what do you want to say in your speech about how to improve school life for all the students?

(There is a short silence.)

Chris: I'm not sure. Every time I think about the speech, my brain seems to just freeze up. All my ideas just evaporate.

(Another short silence.)

30 **Terry:** Well, let's keep working on it. This speech is really important.

Robin: What about sports? The athletic program may be eliminated next year, unless the whole school can find a way to sustain it.

Terry: The principal said athletics are unsustainable. But what if the school could vote to keep some sports by eliminating others—like the ones that cost more?

Robin: Everybody's upset, but nobody's doing much about it.

Chris: If we all worked together and got our families to help, I bet we could raise enough money to keep all the teams. We could start with something like a bake sale.

35 **Robin:** That's a great idea. I think you should put that in your speech.

MAKE INFERENCES Chris says his brain freezes when he thinks about the speech, but at other times in the dialogue, he easily shares his ideas about the teasing problem and about school sports. What inference can you make about Chris and what he is like when he's not nervous about speaking?

PARAPHRASE How would you paraphrase Chris's idea of how to solve the problem with school athletics?

COMPARE AND CONTRAST CHARACTERS How is Terry's idea of what to do about athletics different from Chris's idea? What difference in their characters does this suggest?

COMPARE AND CONTRAST CHARACTERS
How are Terry and Robin alike in what they are trying to do in their meeting with Chris? How are they different in how they are trying to do it?

MAKE INFERENCES Robin uses the word *arrogant* in conversation. What can you infer about Robin for using this word and knowing what it means?

SUMMARIZE When you summarize, you retell the main points about a topic in shorter form. How could you summarize what Terry and Robin say about giving a speech?

Terry: Hey, let's think about something else for a minute. We need a poster design! I was thinking of a stars-and-stripes background with a portrait of you in front.

Chris: A portrait of me?

Robin: I don't think you need a portrait. It might make you seem . . . too proud. Confidence is good, but you don't want to seem arrogant.

Chris: I definitely don't want to seem arrogant.

40 **Robin:** I don't think you have to worry about that. You never act like you think you're more important than other people.

Chris: Do I really have to give a speech?

Terry: If you don't give a speech, how can you win the election? Students need to feel like they know you, or they won't vote for you!

Chris: I don't know how I'm going to do this.

Robin: Maybe you could practice speaking by talking about the school athletics problem, and we can help you.

45 **Terry:** You should stand at the podium.

Robin: You don't have to speak too loudly, because there'll be a microphone at the podium.

Chris: (*Looking down, reading in a dull voice.*) Ladies and gentlemen, I'm Chris for president.

Terry: You can just say 'Good afternoon' to begin your speech. Each candidate will be introduced before speaking, so you won't need to introduce yourself.

Robin: I have to go home in half an hour.

50 **Chris:** I still don't think you should have to give a speech to be elected.

Scene 2

Terry, Robin, and Chris sit outside school, under a tree.

Chris: That speech was a disaster.

Terry: Yes, it was.

Robin: It didn't start off very well, that's true. But you really tried.

Chris: It's just my luck that our washing machine broke this week. The only clothes I could wear for the speech were old.

55 **Terry:** One green sock and one orange sock. That got a lot of attention from the audience.

Robin: Especially with your pant legs too short. I felt so bad for you.

Chris: It was really embarrassing. But the worst thing was that I was the last person to speak. I got more and more nervous while I listened to the other speeches.

Robin: When you walked up to the podium, I didn't see your speech in your hand. Then I realized you might have lost it. I started looking, but the principal told me to find my seat.

> **DRAMA: SCENES** A new scene in a play often shows a shift in the time and place where the action is happening. How have the time and place shifted at the start of Scene 2? How does this shift move the plot forward?

SEQUENCE OF EVENTS
Chris says his speech was a disaster. What sequence of events caused him to say that? How does this sequence of events add to the conflict of the play?

SUMMARIZE A summary of the first scene in this play might be "A candidate for class president meets with two campaign managers to practice his speech. The campaign managers discover he has stage fright and try to help him prepare as best they can." How would you summarize the second scene of the play?

Chris: I just panicked looking at all those faces! I forgot everything about my speech when I was standing at the podium. So I looked down to remind myself, and I didn't even have the paper! So I took a bunch of big, deep breaths to calm down, like you showed me yesterday. But the audience started laughing at me.

60 **Robin:** They weren't laughing at you, exactly—

Terry: It was your breath, aimed right at the microphone. When you took the deep breaths, it sounded like a jet plane or something. How did the water get knocked over?

Chris: My mouth was really dry, and everybody was laughing, so I reached for the water on the table behind the podium. But I was shaking by then, and I knocked it over by accident.

Terry: You could have left the spill until later. Some students thought you just gave up on the speech completely when you left the stage to look for a sponge.

Robin: You were gone for two whole minutes. I was afraid the principal was going to give up on you.

65 **Chris:** I guess I should have given up on either the speech or the spill! I can't believe I tripped on the microphone cord when I came back with the paper towels.

Robin: You're lucky that you're okay—I thought you hit your face when you fell against the podium!

Chris: No. It was more like a hug. An uncomfortable flying hug that I gave the podium while half the school laughed at me. But I wasn't hurt.

Terry: I didn't realize the microphone fell until you picked it up and tried it. I could tell it was broken when you put it down and started shouting the rest of your speech.

Robin: Even though you were shouting, the kids liked your speech. They really liked what you said about how we should all care about each other. It was a strong message. It made them really like you.

70 **Chris:** Thanks.

Terry: Now that you've been elected class president, you know what you're going to have to do, right?

Chris: No, what's that?

Terry: Make more speeches.

The End

MAKE INFERENCES What inference can you make about why Chris was elected class president? What details in the text support your inference?

DRAMA: ACTS Long dramas are usually made up of several acts. Each act may include several scenes that together tell a portion of the story. Acts are often separated by major shifts in time or setting. Short dramas often have only one act. If this play were one act in a longer drama, what might happen in the next act?

Comprehension Check

Think about the structure of "Stage Fright." The play begins with a problem. The problem is developed in Scene 1. It reaches a climax in Scene 2, and then the problem is resolved at the end of the play. Complete the chart below by describing how this structure is developed in the play.

The Structure of "Stage Fright"	
the problem	
how the problem is developed in Scene 1	
how the problem reaches a climax in Scene 2	
how the problem is resolved	

Vocabulary

Use the word map below to help you define and use one of the highlighted vocabulary words from the Share and Learn selection you are about to read or another word you choose.

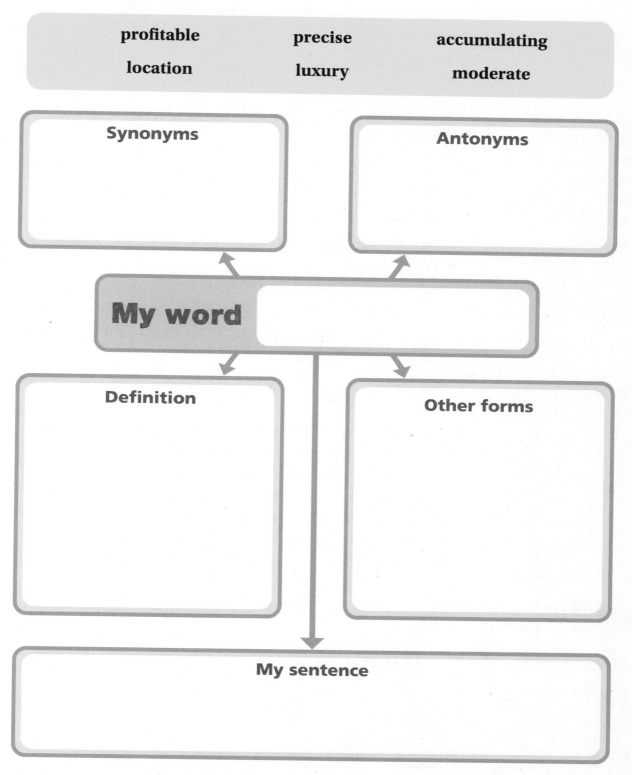

profitable   precise   accumulating

location   luxury   moderate

Synonyms

Antonyms

My word

Definition

Other forms

My sentence

Consider ▶ Is money the most important thing there is?

How does someone learn what is really valuable in life?

Heave, Ho!

Cast of Characters

Landsman, a young sailor on his first long voyage
Captain Hardtack, the captain of the ship
Mr. Petty, the ship's first mate

Act I

A merchant sailing ship prepares for a voyage at a colonial wharf.

CITE EVIDENCE What evidence in the text shows that the captain thinks more about making money than about the safety of his ship and crew?

1   **Petty:** Captain Hardtack, sir. We have tar, planks, and rope aboard.

Captain: Very well, Mr. Petty. Go and oversee the crew. *(Mr. Petty exits.)* Look at this valuable merchandise, roasting in the morning sun . . . we must get it aboard quickly, before it is damaged. . . . You, there! Landsman! *(Landsman enters.)*

Landsman: Yes, Captain—sir! I've come up from the ship's hold, where there is water up to my toes! We're sinking!

Captain: Oh, calm yourself. Let your captain decide if his ship is sunk! It is a wooden ship, Landsman. It always takes a little water in between the planks. It is your first voyage, and here is your first task—come, look. Here are barrels of dried salted codfish, which we will carry to the southern islands. We must stow as many as we can. The more codfish, the more profitable our voyage will be. You must keep a precise count of the barrels as the sailors load them. Take care that your count is exactly correct.

5   **Landsman:** There are a great many barrels, sir.

Captain: Yes, and each of them valuable! The salted cod will be traded for molasses. I shall make a handsome profit from it. The barrels must be handled carefully and packed tightly. Look to your duty!

Landsman: Aye, Captain! (*Landsman exits. Mr. Petty enters.*)

Petty: Captain, it seems that we are accumulating more water in the hold than usual. It is nearly up to my ankles.

Captain: Order the sailors to bail it out with the buckets, Mr. Petty.

10   **Petty:** There are only two bailing buckets aboard, sir.

Captain: Can you find the location of the leak?

Petty: No, sir. There is no single, large leak. There may be many small ones. Perhaps we should check over the ship before we sail, sir?

Captain: Many a ship has sailed the world with a few inches of water in the hold, Mr. Petty! There will be time and money for repairs when we return. Why, we shall sail a golden ship, then!

Petty: Indeed, sir, we all hope to make good earnings on this voyage. (*Aside.*) But all the molasses in the world cannot repair a ship that is lost to the depths of the sea.

15   **Captain:** Our ship was made for the sea, and the sea shall float her home again, Mr. Petty.

COMPARE AND CONTRAST Mr. Petty and Captain Hardtack disagree about how to deal with the condition of the ship. How are their views different on this topic? On what topic do they have similar views?

_____

_____

_____

MAKE INFERENCES Why does the captain say they will "sail a golden ship" when they return from their journey?

_____

_____

_____

Petty: Yes . . . if the sails can hold the wind, sir. The deckhands tell me much of the rope is worn and weak. When we are under full sail, the ropes may break. Perhaps we should replace them?

Captain: Rope is expensive, Mr. Petty. We shall not replace ropes that are still perfectly useful. And we must sail, Mr. Petty! We have not gathered here for the reconstruction of the ship!

Petty: Aye, Captain.

Captain: Now, go and order the lifeboats to be lowered. We shall tow them behind the ship so that more barrels may be put in their places on the deck. Then have the crew make ready the sails.

20 **Petty:** Aye, aye, sir. *(Mr. Petty exits.)*

Captain: *(To himself.)* Hm. I must send the boy Landsman to purchase buckets before we sail. But the wind is calling us, and the weather is fair. When I close my eyes, I smell sweet molasses, and shining coins pour into my hands like falling water. I shall make this my last voyage and live out my days in luxury, like an emperor! The crew worries over ship and rope now. But wait until they are paid their part! Then they will sing the praises of this good ship, and its captain, too.

(Landsman enters.)

Landsman: Captain, sir, the last of the barrels is coming aboard.

Captain: Very good! Let us waste no time! *(Calling out.)* Mr. Petty, where are you?

Landsman: Do you think the ship is fit for the voyage, sir?

25 **Captain:** Landsman, go find Mr. Petty and tell him the time has come.

Act II, Scene 1

(The ship at sea. Captain Hardtack stands on deck. Landsman enters.)

Landsman: Captain Hardtack, the lifeboats are sitting low in the water behind us. They are heavy with water from the spray of the sea. I fear the rope that tows them will break, and the boats will be lost.

Captain: Have the deckhands haul them in and bail them out, then, Landsman.

(Mr. Petty enters.)

Petty: Captain, the topsail is flying free, sir—the ropes have broken, as the crew feared they would.

Captain: Broken? In this pleasant, moderate wind? Have the crew replace the ropes, then. *(Mr. Petty exits.)* A fair wind blows, but my ship scarcely moves! It is as if we were sailing through a sea of porridge. I wonder if the crew ever bailed out the ship. *(He thinks for a moment.)* Oh, dear! I never sent the boy to purchase more bailing buckets. Perhaps I should have taken more care . . . perhaps my impatience has gotten the better of me. What shall I do now? *(He thinks for a moment.)* I will order the ship's carpenter to build buckets from wood or have the sailors make them with cloth and tar.

(Mr. Petty enters.)

DRAMA: ACTS How does the setting change from Act I to Act II of the play?

_____

_____

_____

SEQUENCE OF EVENTS What sequence of events causes the captain to think that he should have taken more care?

_____

_____

_____

THEME The captain says that his impatience has gotten the better of him. What does this suggest might be the theme, or the message, of the play?

_____

_____

_____

SEQUENCE OF EVENTS
What events lead up to the captain's decision to turn the ship around and head back to port?

_____

_____

_____

COMPARE AND CONTRAST How does the captain's attitude change after the lifeboats are lost? In what way does it stay the same?

_____

_____

_____

30 **Petty:** Captain, one of the bailing buckets has broken, and we have but one left. It is not enough for the crew to keep up with the leaks in the hold, and the seawater grows deeper. It is up to my waist.

(Landsman enters.)

Landsman: Captain, the crew hauled the lifeboats in to bail them out, but there was nothing to bail them with, sir. So they let them go, and when the rope was stretched out, it snapped! We've lost our lifeboats!

(The captain puts his hands to his head and stands silently for a moment.)

Captain: There is not enough time to build bailing buckets. *(He sighs heavily and then talks distractedly to himself.)* It seems that perhaps I have made a series of bad decisions. How can this be? I, who have been sailing for thirty years? I, Captain Hardtack, the most successful captain of them all? *(Addressing the others.)* I suppose that we must return to port. Mr. Petty, turn the ship around. And be quick about it. We must make our repairs quickly and set off again. The molasses awaits us!

Petty: Aye, sir. *(Mr. Petty exits.)*

Landsman: Do you think we will make it back to port, sir?

35 **Captain:** We are only an hour's sail away, Landsman.

Landsman: If the ship sinks, we could empty the codfish barrels, tie them together with rope, and float upon them, sir.

Captain: Do not say such a thing, Landsman! We shall not sink or waste any goods as valuable as those! WE shall not sink. We SHALL not sink. . . . We shall NOT . . . *(He pauses.)* Go and see how deep the water is in the hold.

Landsman: Aye! *(He runs off.)*

(Mr. Petty enters.)

Petty: Now that we have turned about, the wind is in our faces, sir.

40 **Captain:** Yes, and it grows stronger. Let us hope that our bow keeps above the waves.

Petty: The crew asks for more buckets, sir, to bail with.

Captain: There are none, Mr. Petty.

Petty: Then . . . we shall sink! We are lost, as I feared. We shall all drown!

Captain: Mr. Petty! Let your captain decide if his ship is sunk!

(Landsman enters.)

45 **Landsman:** Captain, the hold is full of water! It is over my head! The swell of the sea is making the barrels break loose!

Petty: And now look! The weight of the water in the ship forces our bow deeper and deeper into the waves. In a few minutes, the water will be over the deck.

Captain: *(Alarmed.)* Yes, I feel the ship beginning to founder . . . we shall sink . . . we cannot return to port in time, against the wind. Landsman! Mr. Petty! Have the crew bring the barrels of codfish to the deck and pour their contents into the sea. Then have them close the barrels tightly and tie them together with new rope. We must abandon ship and float upon the barrels until we are rescued.

COMPARE AND CONTRAST How do Mr. Petty and Landsman react similarly to the situation the ship is in? In what way are their reactions different?

PARAPHRASE Paraphrase what the captain tells Mr. Petty to do with the codfish.

Act II, Scene 2

SUMMARIZE
Summarize the events in "Heave, Ho!"

(Landsman, the captain, and Mr. Petty ride the ocean swell atop the raft of barrels. Landsman uses a piece of a plank to paddle.)

Petty: Who will rescue us, sir?

Captain: The merchant ship that sails along this route. *(Pointing.)* There. I can already see it on the horizon. We shall be rescued by my old rival, Captain Fussbudget. Ah, well, . . . he is a good fellow and will take care of us.

Petty: Perhaps it would have been better to delay and make the needed repairs, after all.

Captain: Your point is taken, Mr. Petty. *(There is a moment of silence.)* I have lost my fortune and my ship. But Landsman, if it were not for your quick thinking, we might have lost a great deal more than that! Some things are more important than money. I shall take greater care in the future.

THEME What is the theme, or message, of the play?

DRAMA: SCENES How does the last scene of the play fit into the plot of the drama?

The End

Anchor Standard Discussion Questions

Discuss the following questions with your peer group. Then record your answers in the space provided.

1. Captain Hardtack talks to himself at various moments during the play. What do these moments reveal about his character? Why do you think he chooses not to share these thoughts with his shipmates? Support your answers with details from the text.

_____

_____

_____

_____

_____

_____

2. If Captain Hardtack were to ask Mr. Petty to sail with him again, do you think Mr. Petty would accept the offer? Do you think Mr. Petty respects Captain Hardtack? Support your answers with details from the text.

_____

_____

_____

_____

_____

Comprehension Check

1. What lesson do you think Captain Hardtack learns in "Heave, Ho!"? Use evidence from the play to support your opinion.

   _____

   _____

   _____

2. What character trait does Landsman possess that is very important to the plot of "Heave, Ho!"? Use evidence from the play to explain Landsman's character trait and how it is important in the story.

   _____

   _____

   _____

3. How does the sequence of events in Act II, Scene 1 help to build humor and dramatic interest in the play? Use specific evidence from the text in your answer.

   _____

   _____

   _____

Read On Your Own

Read another drama, "Bright Mistakes," independently. Apply what you learned in this lesson and check your understanding.

Writing Fictional Narratives

What do you think is happening in this picture? What do you think might happen next in the story this picture illustrates? Is this something that could happen in the real world of today, or could it only happen in an imaginary world? If you were writing the story, what kind of world would you want to tell about? What characters would you invent? What would happen to them? Would they face danger? What would they say to one another? Think about how you would use your imagination to create your own fictional narrative.

ESSENTIAL QUESTION

What makes a fictional narrative interesting?

What's a Fictional Narrative?

Think about exciting stories or novels you have read. Some of them may have included imaginary creatures or extinct animals that come back to life. Some of them may have taken place in an unfamiliar setting, like outer space or under the sea. Any of these possibilities, and many more, could happen in a fictional narrative.

In a **fictional narrative**, you tell a story that you make up. The flow chart below describes some ways to make your fictional narrative interesting.

Beginning
Introduce the characters, the setting, and the problem that the characters face.

Middle
Develop your fictional story. Use narrative techniques such as description, dialogue, and pacing to make your story convincing. Use vivid details in the narration to create mental pictures for the reader.

Ending
Bring your fictional narrative to a satisfying close that solves the problem.

Let's look at a fictional narrative.

Analyze a Mentor Text

This is an example of an interesting fifth-grade fictional narrative. Read it and then complete the activities in the boxes as a class.

Simon and the Spaceship

Clang! Crash! Cr-r-r-ack! Simon looked around him as the dozens of metal pieces littering the floor spoke to him. *No one can say I have a quiet job,* he thought. *Restoring spaceships is a noisy business. And what should I do about that letter I found? Should I tell someone, or keep it a secret?*

Simon worked for the Wyrium Planet Museum. He restored spaceships from other planets that had crashed onto Wyrium. He loved walking slowly through the big main hall of the museum. There were old spaceships from as far back as 2250 and shiny new ones, like the one he was restoring now. The old spaceships told him stories from the history of star exploration, and Simon loved to learn from them.

But the ship he was working on now was no ordinary spaceship. It was from the Battle of the Brown Hills, from just six months ago. For three days, pilots from Wyrium had fought off invaders from an unknown galaxy. The invading force had been a raging storm. Although it was a close fight, in the end, the invaders lost and were all killed. The pilots of Wyrium were heroes!

Simon wanted to do an excellent job on this spaceship, to honor the pilots who had shot it down. Before he put the spaceship back together, he polished each piece until it shone like a sun. But yesterday he had found something strange. As he was polishing the spaceship's control panel, he had found a piece of paper stuck behind it.

Simon had unfolded the paper and was surprised to see that the writing on it was in his own language. As he read the scribbled note, his heart grew heavy as lead. "To the people of your planet," it began. "I am writing this in haste. Your planes are shooting at us, and I am certain we will all die. But we come in peace."

BEGINNING The writer captures the reader's interest by describing the sounds that the metal pieces make. The beginning also introduces the problem the main character faces. Underline the main character's thoughts about the problem.

MIDDLE The writer uses vivid description to help the reader picture the narrative. Circle words in paragraph 2 that bring the narrative to life.

MIDDLE The writer uses the narrative technique of flashback to tell what happened the day before and explain the problem Simon faces. Underline the sentences that tell what happened the day before.

What's a Fictional Narrative? **47**

MIDDLE The writer tells part of the story through the words of a letter. The author also uses dialogue, or the words characters speak, to add interest and explain the resolution of the story.

ENDING Writers make sure the ending of the narrative solves the problem that the characters face in a satisfying way. Underline sentences in the narrative that give a satisfying ending.

"We seek your help, for the people of our planet have run out of food and are starving. Even if we die, please help them so they may live." The note was signed "Captain Rosario Garcia."

Simon hadn't known what to do. Should he tell someone about the note? If he did, the pilots of Wyrium would no longer be heroes. But if he kept the note to himself, people in a faraway galaxy could die. Now, as he thought again about the letter, Simon felt numb and cold like ice, but he was also sweating. The spaceship was no longer just a silent, battered vehicle. It was a messenger. It cried out to him. He had to act.

The museum director's office was on the first floor of the building. The director, Sandra Cooke, greeted him warmly, with a smile. "You should see this," he said. "I found it in one of the spaceships." His hand was shaking as he gave her the note.

He watched Ms. Cooke's face grow serious as she read. Then she glanced at him and picked up the phone. In a few minutes she hung up and said, "That was the director of national security. He is going to find out where this spaceship came from and prepare to send rockets with food to that planet."

"What about our pilot heroes?" Simon asked.

"This note changes the story of the Battle of the Brown Hills," Ms. Cooke said. "But if we're lucky, maybe we will all be heroes anyway."

Simon smiled. He was glad he had made the right decision.

Think About It ▶ What aspect of the narrative do you like best?

Do you think the reader is likely to find the narrative interesting? Why or why not?

Vocabulary Study: Figurative Language

Figurative language is language that makes writing more vivid by comparing one thing to another in a surprising way. Three important types of figurative language are simile, metaphor, and personification.

A **simile** compares two unlike things using the word *like* or *as*: *The sun was like a ball of fire*. A **metaphor** compares two things without using *like* or *as*: *The sun was a ball of fire*. **Personification** gives an object human qualities, such as feelings and actions: *The sun smiled on the earth*. Work with your class or a partner to complete the chart below.

Sentence	Type of Figurative Language
Her heartbeat was a hammer pounding.	Metaphor
The teakettle screamed from the stove.	
His hair was like soft moonlight.	
The dog's fur was a blanket he wore year-round.	
The rocks grumbled as they shifted.	
My face was red as a beet.	

Look back at the fictional narrative on pages 47–48. Find examples of each type of figurative language, and write the phrases or sentences in the chart.

Type of Figurative Language	Example
Simile	
Metaphor	
Personification	

Writing Process

Now that you have read and analyzed a fictional narrative, you are going to create your own by following these steps of the writing process.

1. Get Ready: Brainstorm Think about the main character and events. What does the main character look like? What problem will he or she face? Decide whether you want to write about things that could really happen or about things that could happen only in a fantasy.

2. Organize Use a graphic organizer to plan your fictional narrative.

3. Draft Create the first draft of your fictional narrative.

4. Peer Review Work with a partner to evaluate and improve your draft.

5. Revise Use suggestions from your peer review to revise your fictional narrative.

6. Edit Check your work carefully for spelling, punctuation, and grammar errors.

7. Publish Create a final version of your fictional narrative.

Writing Assignment

In this lesson, you will write your own fictional narrative. As you create this piece, remember the elements of the mentor text that were most interesting and effective. Read the following assignment.

> Write a story about someone who learns something that totally changes his or her view of a situation.

1. Get Ready: Brainstorm

The first step in writing a fictional narrative is to choose your main character and setting.

Here's how the author of the mentor fictional narrative brainstormed character and setting.

Character	
Who is the main character?	Simon, a museum worker
What makes this character special?	He restores spaceships that tell the history of space exploration.
Setting	
Where and when does the narrative take place?	In a museum on the planet Wyrium, in the future.
What is unique about the setting of the story?	The people of Wyrium recently fought a battle against ships from another galaxy.

Try It! Use a Brainstorming Graphic Organizer

Now use the chart below to help brainstorm topics for your own fictional narrative.

Characters	
Who is the main character?	
How would you describe his or her personality?	
What makes this character special?	
Setting	
Where and when does the narrative take place?	
What is unique about this setting?	

Brainstorm Ideas for Your Narrative

Next, think of a problem your character will face in the narrative. You can use a graphic organizer to think about how the character and setting are related to the problem. Here is how the author of the mentor text used the graphic organizer.

PROBLEM Your character should face a problem. Make clear what the problem is and why it is a problem.

> ## Problem
> While restoring an enemy spaceship from a famous battle, Simon learns that the people in the spaceship were not attacking but seeking help for their starving people. Simon must decide whether to share this new information or keep it to himself. If he shares the information, his planet's pilots will no longer seem like heroes.

NARRATIVE DEVELOPMENT Plan how the problem will be developed and how you will unfold the events of the plot to make the story interesting. Outline the use of narrative techniques, such as dialogue.

> ## Narrative Development
> Simon discovers a letter hidden in the spaceship. It tells him that the others were not really attacking.
>
> Simon worries about what to do, but then shows the letter to the museum director. In their dialogue, she arranges to send help to the faraway planet.

RESOLUTION Plan how the problem will be resolved and how to make the ending satisfying for the reader.

> ## Resolution
> The museum director says that perhaps they will all be heroes of a different kind.

Try It!   Use a Graphic Organizer for Brainstorming

Now use the graphic organizer below to brainstorm the problem and how you will develop the narrative and resolution of your fictional piece.

Problem

Narrative Development

Resolution

2. Organize

You are almost ready to begin a draft of your fictional narrative. Create a story map by extending the graphic organizer you used during brainstorming. Add details about how you will develop the narrative. You can then refer to the story map as you work through your draft. The writer of the mentor text completed this story map.

BEGINNING Begin by introducing the setting, the main character, and the problem.

MIDDLE Include events that show how the problem developed and how the character deals with the problem. Include vivid details and dialogue to make your writing interesting.

ENDING Think of an ending that will resolve the problem and be satisfying for the reader.

Character
Simon: worker who restores spaceships in the museum

Setting
The Wyrium Planet Museum

The future

Problem
While restoring a spaceship from a famous battle, Simon learns that the people in the spaceship were not attacking but seeking help for their starving people. Simon must decide whether to share this new information or keep it to himself.

Narrative Development
If Simon shares the information he has discovered, the heroic pilots of his planet will look bad. He tries to go back to work, but he can't ignore the note he found. He decides to share it with the director, Ms. Cooke. As part of their dialogue, Ms. Cooke calls the director of national security, who makes a plan to ship food to the planet that sent the spaceships.

Resolution
Simon asks Ms. Cooke what will happen to the pilot heroes. She tells him they will all be heroes if the plan to feed the starving people succeeds.

Try It!

Organize Your Fictional Narrative

Now use the graphic organizer below to organize the narration and resolution for your draft.

Character

Setting

Problem

Narrative Development

Resolution

3. Draft

Now it is time to begin the first draft of your fictional narrative. Remember, your draft does not have to be perfect! This is the time to use your notes, get your story down in some sort of organized way, and have fun. You will have time to revise your writing later. Start by drafting your fictional narrative on a computer or on a separate sheet of paper. Make your characters come to life!

Writer's Craft: Using Transitional Words and Phrases

Transitional words and phrases tie together the sentences and paragraphs of your writing. Transitional words and phrases can show time order, causes and effects, place, similarities and differences, additional ideas, and degree of importance.

Type of Transition	Examples
Time clues	after, afterward, at last, before, finally, last week, meanwhile, next, since, soon, when
Causes and effects	as a result, because, due to, so that, therefore, thus
Place clues	above, around, beside, down, over, there, under
Similarities and differences	like, similarly, although, but, however, nevertheless, in contrast, instead, unlike
Additional ideas	also, another, furthermore, in addition, too
Degree of importance	above all, better, best, equally important, most important, strongest, worse, worst

The author of the mentor text uses transitional words and phrases in paragraph 3.

TRANSITIONAL WORDS AND PHRASES Read this section of the mentor text. Underline the transitional words and phrases.

But the ship he was working on now was no ordinary spaceship. It was from the Battle of the Brown Hills, from just six months ago. For three days, pilots from Wyrium had fought off invaders from an unknown galaxy. The invading force had been a raging storm. Although it was a close fight, in the end, the invaders lost and were all killed. The pilots of Wyrium were heroes!

Try It!   Write Your First Draft

On a computer or a separate sheet of paper, continue the draft of your fictional narrative. Remember to use transitional words and phrases to tie your writing together. Use this drafting checklist to help you as you write.

✔ A good beginning gets your reader's attention. You can begin with dialogue, a dramatic statement, or a compelling action.

✔ Introduce the main character and setting at the beginning of the narrative.

✔ Develop the narrative around the problem the main character faces.

✔ Show how your character deals with the problem in the middle of your story.

✔ Show how the problem is resolved in the ending.

✔ Use transitional words and phrases to tie the events together.

Tips for Writing Your First Draft

- Write down key descriptions and pieces of dialogue before you begin writing. Sometimes this is a great warm-up to get you started.

- Think about a difficult situation that you have been in. And remember, in your narrative, *anything* can happen!

- Sometimes visualizing helps writers understand their characters. If you get stuck, try drawing a picture.

4. Peer Review

After you finish your draft, you can work with a partner to review each other's drafts. Here is a draft of the mentor text. Read it with your partner. Together, answer the questions in the boxes. Then we'll see how the writer's classmate evaluated the draft.

An Early Draft:

BEGINNING In the draft, the writer does not make clear what Simon is doing. The beginning is also not very interesting. What revisions would you make?

MIDDLE The narrative doesn't show Simon as having a problem. It also could use more description to make it come to life. What revisions would you make?

ENDING The ending is not very satisfying. It needs to show how Simon's feelings about the letter are resolved. Also, some dialogue and more details of the interaction between Simon and Ms. Cooke would make it stronger. What dialogue and details would you add?

Simon and the Spaceship

Simon looked around him at dozens of metal pieces littering the floor. He worked for the Wyrium Planet Museum. He restored spaceships from other planets that had crashed onto Wyrium. Some were really old, and some were new, like the one he was restoring now.

This spaceship was left over from the Battle of the Brown Hills. For three days, pilots from Wyrium had fought off invaders from an unknown galaxy. In the end, the invaders lost. The pilots of Wyrium were heroes.

Simon wanted to do an extra-good job of restoring this spaceship. He was busy polishing the spaceship's control panel when, suddenly, a piece of it came loose and clattered to the floor. He bent to pick it up and saw that a piece of paper was stuck to the back of the panel piece.

Simon unfolded the paper and read the note. "To the people of your planet," it began. "I am writing this in haste. Your planes are shooting at us, and I am certain we will all die. But we come in peace. We seek your help, for the people of our planet have run out of food and are starving. Even if we die, please help them so they may live."

Simon took the note to the museum director's office. The director, Sandra Cooke, greeted him with a smile. Simon handed her the note.

Ms. Cooke read the note and called the director of national security, who promised to send rockets with food to the planet that the spaceship came from.

An Example Peer Review Form

This peer review form gives an example of how a classmate evaluated the draft of the mentor text shown on page 58.

The narrative includes a strong beginning, middle, and ending.	You did a good job of introducing who Simon is.
The beginning introduces the main character, setting, and problem.	You could improve your fictional narrative by showing what Simon is doing as the narrative opens.
The plot develops from the problem the character faces.	You did a good job of telling what was in the note Simon found.
In the middle, the writer shows how the character deals with the problem.	You could improve your fictional narrative by making it clearer that Simon had a serious choice to make concerning what to do with the note.
The writer uses description, dialogue, and transitional words and phrases to bring the narrative to life and to tie the events together.	You did a good job of telling the events of the narrative in order and using transitional words and phrases.
	You could improve your fictional narrative by adding dialogue and more description.
The ending shows how the problem is resolved.	You did a good job of telling how the starving strangers could be helped.
The writer makes the ending satisfying to the reader.	You could improve your fictional narrative by showing how Simon's feelings about the letter are resolved.

Try It! Peer Review with a Partner

Now you are going to work with a partner to review each other's fictional narrative drafts. You will use the peer review form below. If you need help, look back at the mentor text writer's peer review form for suggestions.

| The narrative includes a strong beginning, middle, and ending. | You did a good job of |
| The beginning introduces the main character, setting, and problem. | You could improve your fictional narrative by |

| The plot develops from the problem the character faces. | You did a good job of |
| In the middle, the writer shows how the character deals with the problem. | You could improve your fictional narrative by |

| The writer uses description, dialogue, and transitional words and phrases to bring the narrative to life and to tie the events together. | You did a good job of |
| | You could improve your fictional narrative by |

| The ending shows how the problem is resolved. | You did a good job of |
| The writer makes the ending satisfying to the reader. | You could improve your fictional narrative by |

Try It! **Record Key Peer Review Comments**

Now it's time for you and your partner to share your comments with each other. Listen to your partner's feedback, and write down the key comments in the left column. Then write some ideas for improving your draft in the right column.

My review says that the beginning	I will
My review says that the main character	I will
My review says that the setting	I will
My review says that the problem the character faces	I will
My review says that the development of the narrative	I will
My review says that the ending	I will

Use the space below to write anything else you notice about your draft that you think you can improve.

5. Revise

In this step of the writing process, you work on parts of your draft that need improvement. Use the peer review form that your classmate completed to help you. Also use your own ideas about how to improve each part of your fictional narrative. This checklist includes some things to think about as you get ready to revise.

Revision Checklist

✔ Does my beginning introduce the main character and setting well? Is the problem presented clearly?

✔ Does the middle show events that develop naturally from the problem?

✔ Does the middle show how the main character deals with the problem?

✔ Does the ending resolve the problem? Does it satisfy the reader?

✔ Do I use transitional words and phrases to tie the narrative together?

✔ Do I use sensory language to make my narrative come to life?

Writer's Craft: Using Sensory Language

Using words that appeal to the five senses makes your fictional narrative lively and more convincing. For example, instead of writing "The plane flew overhead," you might write "The plane roared across the blue sky." Instead of saying flowers are "nice," you might say they are "fragrant and delicate." Now look at the mentor text for examples of sensory language.

SENSORY LANGUAGE
Sensory language appeals to the senses of hearing, sight, smell, taste, and touch. Underline sensory language in this paragraph.

How does sensory language help you understand how Simon is feeling?

_____

_____

_____

> … Simon felt numb and cold like ice, but he was also sweating. The spaceship was no longer just a silent, battered vehicle. It was a messenger. It cried out to him. He had to act.
>
> The museum director's office was on the first floor of the building. The director, Sandra Cooke, greeted him warmly, with a smile. "You should see this," he said. "I found it in one of the spaceships." His hand was shaking as he gave her the note.

Try It!   **Revise Your Fictional Narrative**

Replacing simple words with sensory language is an important part of revising. Practice using sensory language with the following paragraph. Rewrite the paragraph, replacing each underlined word or phrase with a word or phrase that appeals to the senses.

Suddenly a bear <u>came</u> out of the woods. Hilary <u>stood</u> in place and looked at the <u>big</u> animal. Its ribs <u>showed</u> under its <u>uneven</u> coat. The bear made a <u>sad noise</u>. "Poor thing, you're <u>needing food</u>," said Hilary. "Have my <u>good</u> sandwich. It's full of <u>nice</u> honey." She tossed the sandwich to the bear. The bear picked up the sandwich and <u>went</u> into the woods.

_____

_____

_____

_____

Writing Assignment

Now it's time to revise the draft of your fictional narrative. Continue working on a computer or on a separate sheet of paper. Review the assignment below and the checklist to remember what to include.

Write a story about someone who learns something that totally changes his or her view of a situation.

6. Edit

After revising your fictional narrative, you will edit it. When you edit, you read very carefully to find any mistakes. Here's a checklist of some things to look for.

> **Editing Checklist**
>
> ✓ Did you indent each paragraph?
>
> ✓ Are all of your sentences complete? Does each have a subject and a verb?
>
> ✓ Did you begin each sentence with a capital letter?
>
> ✓ Does each sentence end with the correct punctuation?
>
> ✓ Have you used commas correctly?
>
> ✓ Are all of your words spelled correctly?

You can use these editing marks to mark any errors you find.

> ^ Add   ~~delete~~ Delete   ↙↘ Insert quotation marks
>
> ∩ Reverse the order of letters or words
>
> / Change a capital to a lowercase letter
>
> ≡ Change a lowercase to a capital letter

This paragraph from an early draft of the mentor text shows how to use editing marks.

He watched Ms. cooke's face grow serious as she read. Then she glanced at him and picked the phone. In a few minutes she hung up and said, That was the director of national security. He is is going to find out where this spaceship came from and prepare send to Rockets with food to that planet.

Language Focus: Conjunctions, Prepositions, and Interjections

A **conjunction** is a word that connects two words, sentences, or phrases, as in, "I ate soup *and* salad." A **preposition** is a word that links a noun or pronoun to other words in a sentence. It often indicates how things are related in time or space. An **interjection** is a word or phrase used in a way that shows feeling.

Conjunctions	*and, but, or, for, so, nor*
Prepositions	*above, against, around, at, before, behind, between, down, during, for, from, in, into, of, on, until, up, with*
Interjections	*no, oh, really, wait, well, wow, yes*

Conjunction examples:

You **and** I could go hiking.

Herbert wanted to see a movie, **but** Dorie wanted to read.

Preposition examples:

Pippa ate lunch **between** noon and one o'clock.

During his baby sister's nap, Warren stayed **in** his room.

Interjection examples:

Oh, no! I think I left my key at home.

Well, you might have called me.

Simon worked for the Wyrium Planet Museum. He restored spaceships from other planets that had crashed onto Wyrium. He loved walking slowly through the big main hall of the museum. There were old spaceships from as far back as 2250 and shiny new ones, like the one he was restoring now. The old spaceships told him stories from the history of star exploration, and Simon loved to learn from them.

CONJUNCTIONS, PREPOSITIONS, AND INTERJECTIONS Read this section of the mentor text. Underline the conjunctions you see. Draw a box around the prepositions.

Try It!   Language and Editing Practice

Complete each sentence by writing a conjunction, a preposition, or an interjection on each blank line. Use each word from the box only once.

and	Wow!	behind	but	after
before	from	Well,	to	or

1. Maura hid _____ her sister _____ the bedroom curtain.

2. Jermain _____ Alex biked _____ the swimming pool, _____ it was closed.

3. _____ Our team won the game!

4. _____ I'll call you again tomorrow _____ I go to bed.

5. My favorite snack _____ school is a banana _____ an apple.

Now use editing marks to correct the errors in this paragraph.

Tatiana helped her mother bring the groceries into the house.

Gracious, she said when she saw the mess her older brother, Micah, was

making the kitchen. She could see that Micah was cooking their dinner,

or he was using every pan in the kitchen. At this rate, they would be

eating midnight!

Try It! Edit Your Fictional Narrative

Now edit your fictional narrative. Use this checklist and the editing marks you have learned to correct any errors you find.

☐ Did you indent each paragraph?

☐ Are all of your sentences complete? Have you corrected fragments and run-ons?

☐ Did you begin each sentence with a capital letter and end each sentence with the correct punctuation?

☐ Have you used powerful sensory language to appeal to your reader's senses?

☐ Have you used commas correctly?

☐ Have you used transitional words and phrases effectively to link ideas?

☐ Have you used conjunctions, prepositions, and interjections correctly?

Editing Tips

- Read your writing aloud. Listen carefully as you read for stops and pauses. Stops and pauses usually indicate the places where punctuation might go. Ask yourself, "Am I missing any punctuation?"

- Read backward from the end of your writing, one sentence at a time. This may help you catch mistakes you would not notice otherwise.

- Set your writing aside for a day or so before you reread it. Looking at it with fresh eyes may help you see things you missed before.

7. Publish

On a computer or a separate sheet of paper, create a neat final draft of your fictional narrative. Correct all errors that you identified while editing your draft. Be sure to give your fictional narrative an interesting title.

The final step is to publish your fictional narrative. Here are some different ways you might choose to share your work.

- Create a short story collection using your and your classmates' fictional narratives.

- Read your fictional narrative to your class during an "open mic" event.

- Get permission to read your fictional narrative aloud to students from a lower grade.

- Illustrate your fictional narrative with pictures of characters or events.

Technology Suggestions

- Upload your fictional narrative onto your class or school blog.
- Use graphics software to create illustrations for your fictional narrative.

Reading Historical Nonfiction

Look at this model of the ancient city of Tenochtitlán. How do you think this area looks today?

ESSENTIAL QUESTION

How does historical nonfiction help us understand the world today?

Consider ▶ What can we learn from the inventions and cultural practices of ancient civilizations?

What parts of daily life in Tenochtitlán were similar to our lives today?

HISTORICAL NONFICTION

Accounts of real events or people from the past are called historical nonfiction. Unlike fictional stories, these articles or essays are nonfiction because all of the details are true. They are historical because the events happened in the past, whether ten years ago or ten thousand years ago. What real people or events is this historical nonfiction article about?

CHRONOLOGICAL ORDER

Chronological order is the order in which events happen in time. Historical nonfiction is usually organized in chronological order: events are described in the order in which they happened. This is often important for understanding how one event can cause another thing to happen. Look at paragraph 2. Did the Aztec become powerful before or after they settled on a marshy island?

Tenochtitlán:
Life in the Aztec Capital

1   Five centuries ago, Tenochtitlán (teh-nosh-teet-LAHN) was the grandest city in the Americas. It boasted a population of more than 200,000 residents. Its wildly colorful buildings and monuments rivaled those of Europe's great cities. It was also a center of power. The city was the capital of an empire that stretched across Mexico. Although its destruction was sudden and complete, Tenochtitlán has lived on as one of the greatest cities in history.

The founders and builders of Tenochtitlán were the Aztec. In the twelfth century, this group began to move into the Valley of Mexico from what is now northwestern Mexico. Other, more powerful groups already lived in the area. These groups forced the Aztec to move repeatedly. Then, in 1325, the Aztec built a settlement on a marshy island in Lake Texcoco. They could protect themselves there, and they soon grew powerful. Within one hundred years, Tenochtitlán grew into a tremendous city. From there, the Aztec were able to take control of the vast valley surrounding the lake.

And what a stunning city Tenochtitlán was! It featured a mighty central pyramid, as tall as a ten-story building. Monuments, palaces, and parks added splendor. Huge marketplaces were filled with people buying and selling goods from near and far. Long causeways, or raised roads, extended for miles and connected the island with the mainland. Two aqueducts brought fresh water to the island. Canals traversed the area, with canoes transporting people and goods. At the beginning of the sixteenth century, Tenochtitlán surpassed many capitals of Europe in both size and beauty.

Constructing the City

The construction of Tenochtitlán was an amazing feat. The soil it was built on was extremely spongy. The Aztec had to create a special foundation system. Buildings were constructed on platforms to prevent them from sinking into the muck. The nearby areas offered no building materials. Wood and stone had to be brought in from far away. Most remarkably, the city was built without the help of metal tools or wheeled vehicles. Nor did the Aztec use pack animals, such as oxen or horses. Instead, they hauled supplies by hand over great distances.

AUTHOR'S POINT OF VIEW
An author's choice of words often reflects his or her point of view, or attitude, about a topic. An author may be positive and enthusiastic about a topic or may be negative and critical about it. Reread paragraphs 3 and 4 to determine the author's attitude, or point of view, about the Aztec. Does the author have a positive or negative view of the Aztec? Which words tell you the author's viewpoint?

READING MAPS A map is a visual representation of an area showing its physical features, such as cities, roads, or rivers. Maps can often help you understand geographic information better than text alone can. The map on this page shows Tenochtitlán's location on Lake Texcoco and the location of the city's neighbors. What city could be reached the fastest from Tenochtitlán?

Tenochtitlán's many neighbors included both allies and rival groups.

Floating Islands

5   The Aztec built a number of floating islands around the city. These islands were called *chinamitl* (CHEE-nah-MEE-tuhl) in the Aztec language, Náhuatl. They were used to increase the city's farmland. To build one of these floating islands, a mass of small branches and grasses were formed into a raft. The island builders then drove stakes into the ground around the raft's edges. Earth and stones were added to the raft. This sank the base of the new island

Floating islands allowed the Aztec to maximize the amount of farmland in the city.

well below the lake's surface. Fertile soil was then laid on the top, perfect for raising crops. Trees planted along the edge of each island helped hold the land together.

Farming in Tenochtitlán

Most farmers in Tenochtitlán had only small plots of land. On these plots, they grew mainly corn and beans. They also grew squash, sweet potatoes, tomatoes, and chili peppers. Farmers in drier areas on the mainland grew cotton and cactus. Some also grew agave, a plant used to make cloth, sewing needles, and drinks.

Houses and Palaces

Most houses in Tenochtitlán were made of adobe (ah-DOH-bee), or sun-dried bricks. These houses were usually one-room buildings. Aztec families divided the space into separate areas for cooking, eating, and sleeping. Families ate around a central fire. They sat on woven mats. These houses were built in groups, facing a central courtyard. Farmers on the floating islands lived in wooden huts with thatched roofs.

The nobles lived closest to the city's center. These wealthy officials lived in two-story stone houses. Many of these houses had flower beds, pools, and fruit orchards. However, these houses could not compare to the palaces that the Aztec kings lived in. One of the royal palaces in Tenochtitlán had more than three hundred rooms. The grounds around it featured ornate gardens and highly decorated fountains. This palace was also home to the royal zoo. There, one could see eagles, jaguars, snakes, and other animals from throughout the empire.

Aztec Kings

Aztec kings were known as *tlatoani* (tla-toh-AH-nee). This means "great speaker." The king was chosen by a council of four nobles. When a new king was needed, the council would choose the wisest and bravest of the last ruler's brothers, sons, or nephews. The Aztec king had control over the army. However, he relied on local nobles to govern throughout the city and surrounding areas.

10   Aztec kings enjoyed the privileges that came with their power. For example, each day, King Moctezuma II had cooks prepare more than three hundred dishes, from which he chose only a few. Acrobats, jugglers, singers, and dancers performed during the king's meals. Musicians also played day and night in the royal palace.

Aztec kings, such as Moctezuma II, enjoyed tremendous wealth and power.

CONTEXT CLUES You can often figure out the meaning of a word you don't know by looking for clues in the words around it. These context clues can help you understand the unknown word. Look at the sixth sentence in paragraph 8. What context clue can help you figure out the meaning of *ornate*?

INTEGRATING INFORMATION Readers of historical nonfiction often look at multiple sources about a single topic. They then integrate, or combine, the information from these sources to understand the topic more fully. This article describes the power of the Aztec kings. What additional information about the lifestyle of Aztec kings and the luxuries they enjoyed would you want to find in another source?

Education and Professions

Education was highly valued in Aztec society. Aztec children were taught practical skills at home until about age twelve. Boys learned how to fish and handle a canoe from their fathers. Mothers taught their daughters how to spin thread and how to grind corn for tortillas. Manners were also very important and were taught to children at an early age.

At age twelve, the sons of commoners went to live at boarding schools. There they learned how to work in the fields, build roads, and repair canals. They also learned how to become warriors. Both boys and girls went to a "House of Song" from ages twelve to fifteen. There they were taught the songs, dances, and music of the Aztec religion.

The sons of the nobles went to a temple school when they were twelve years old. At these schools, they studied to become priests. Priests were very important and powerful in Aztec society. Students in these schools learned about Aztec customs and the Aztec religion. They also received military training. Few of them knew how to read, but students learned important texts by heart.

As they grew up, young men in Tenochtitlán usually did the same type of work as their fathers. Many worked as builders and stonemasons. Others worked as metalworkers, potters, weavers, and canoe makers. Male commoners also had to serve in the army during times of war. Women worked mostly in the home. They looked after the children and prepared food for their families. Women also wove cloth.

Aztec daughters learned many valuable skills from their mothers.

Goods from throughout the Aztec Empire were traded in Tenochtitlán's bustling markets.

Tenochtitlán's Markets

15   Tenochtitlán featured grand markets full of gold and silver items. One could also find gems, rare feathers, and medicines there. Other merchants sold clothing, pottery, and even live animals. Farmers used the city's canals to bring goods to the markets in canoes. The Aztec had no coins or paper money. Instead, they used rolls of cotton cloth as currency. Some used rare cacao beans as currency as well. These beans were valuable imported goods in Tenochtitlán. Many people also bartered, or exchanged goods directly.

Aztec Food

Most people ate a type of corn cereal for breakfast. Dinners were cooked on a hot stone or a clay griddle. These usually consisted of corn tortillas, sometimes served with chili peppers or tomatoes. Occasionally dinners included small amounts of fish, duck, turkey, or rabbit.

Aztec kings and nobles ate much more fancily. Their meals included deer, turkey, quail, and fish. They also ate tamales, tortillas, and beans. They enjoyed desserts made from tropical fruit. They also drank chocolate drinks made from expensive cacao beans.

CONTEXT CLUES
Paragraph 15 says that the Aztec often used cacao beans or rolls of cotton cloth as currency. What context clues help you understand what *currency* means?

COMPARE AND CONTRAST
Authors sometimes organize their writing by comparing and contrasting information. When they compare, they point out things that are similar. When they contrast, they point out things that are different. On this page, the author describes the food of ordinary Aztec people and contrasts the food of the kings and nobles with it. How was the food of kings and nobles different from the food of the rest of the people?

Aztec Clothing

The clothes people wore in Tenochtitlán depended on their social class. Only rulers and priests could wear turquoise jewelry. Likewise, only nobles and officials were allowed to wear cotton clothes. Commoners made yarn from agave fibers and knitted clothes from this fabric. Women wore skirts and sleeveless blouses. The men wore loincloths and tied capes over their shoulders.

The Aztec Calendars

The Aztec used two different calendars. Their ordinary calendar had 365 days each year, just like the calendar that we use today. This helped people know when to plant crops and to remember when ceremonies would occur. Their religious calendar had only 260 days per year. This year was divided into thirteen months. Thirteen was a sacred number for the Aztec. They believed that a different god or goddess ruled each of the thirteen months.

Writing System

20   Aztec writing was not done with letters. Instead, the Aztec used symbols known as glyphs. These small pictures could be combined to convey a message. Writing skills were rare. Specially trained craftsmen called scribes performed most writing. The Aztec made paper from tree bark. A long strip of this paper was folded repeatedly to form a type of book called a codex. Some of the Aztec codices (plural of codex) survive today and help us understand this ancient culture.

Rather than using an alphabet, the Aztec created a system of pictorial symbols to express ideas in writing.

The Aztec Legacy

The Aztec civilization came to an abrupt end after the Spanish invaded Mexico in the sixteenth century. The Spanish destroyed Tenochtitlán. They founded Mexico City on top of the city's ruins. However, many aspects of Aztec culture remain visible to us today. The jaguar was a sacred animal for the Aztec. This remains a popular symbol in modern Mexico. Many words we commonly use in English come from the Aztec language, including *avocado, chocolate, coyote,* and *tomato.* The Mexican national soccer team plays its home games in Estadio Azteca, or Aztec Stadium. And the Mexican flag features an eagle with a snake in its mouth, perched on a cactus. This image comes from an important Aztec myth about the founding of Tenochtitlán.

SUMMARIZE To summarize means to briefly retell the main points of something you have read. Summarizing can help you organize and remember the most important ideas in a text. Look back at paragraph 21. How would you summarize this paragraph in one sentence?

GLOSSARY A glossary is a list of difficult or special words and their meanings, often placed in the back of a book. A glossary might give one of these meanings for *legacy*: *1. Property that is inherited; 2. Something passed down from earlier generations; 3. Status acquired through birth.*

Which meaning of *legacy* best fits the way the word is used on this page?

Comprehension Check

Look back at "Tenochtitlán: Life in the Aztec Capital." How was life different for Aztec commoners from how it was for the powerful nobles? Complete the chart below to show the ways that daily life differed between these groups.

Commoners	Nobles
lived in one-room houses	lived in two-story houses

Vocabulary

Use the word map below to help you define and use one of the highlighted vocabulary words from the Share and Learn selection you are about to read or another word you choose.

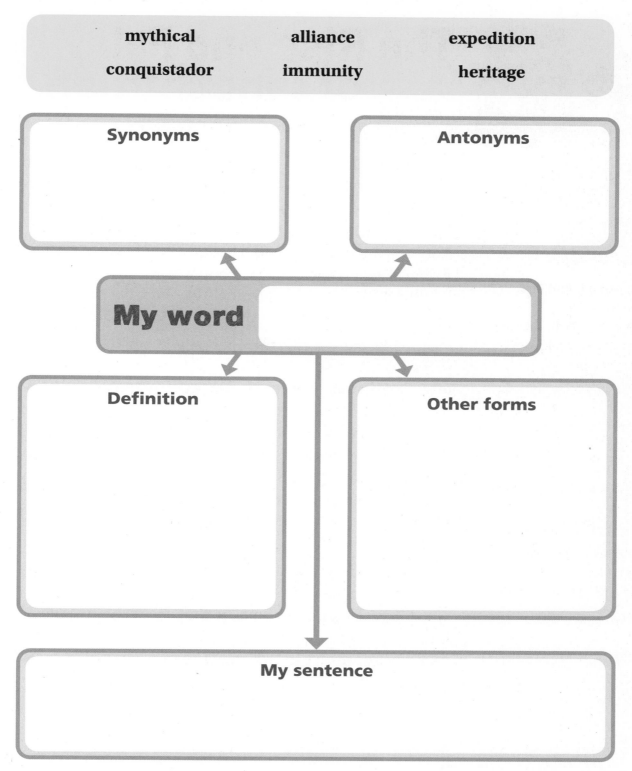

mythical   alliance   expedition

conquistador   immunity   heritage

Synonyms

Antonyms

My word

Definition

Other forms

My sentence

Consider ► How did the growth of the Aztec Empire affect life across central Mexico?

Why did life there change so abruptly after the Spanish arrived?

The Rise and Fall of Tenochtitlán

The Aztec image of an eagle clutching a serpent remains a powerful symbol of Mexico today.

Aztec Origins

1   In the twelfth century, a group of hunters moved into the highland plateau region known today as the Valley of Mexico. This group called themselves the Mexica (meh-SHEE-kah). To others in the area, they were known as the Aztec. In the Náhuatl language, the word *Aztec* means "the people from Aztlán." Legend told that this group had left their home on the mythical island city of Aztlán. They were forced to wander in search of a new home.

   In 1299, this group arrived at Chapultepec Hill, a location that is now in Mexico City. The Tepanec people living in this area allowed the Aztec to stay. The Aztec promised that they would work for the Tepanec as laborers and serve in their army. However, the Tepanec attitude soon changed, and the Aztec were forced to leave. They moved to the southeastern side of Lake Texcoco, near the town of Culhuacán. The Aztec soon made enemies with their new neighbors. They were forced to flee again. They took refuge on a marshy island in the middle of the lake.

   An Aztec legend said that the people would know where to settle when they saw an eagle, perched on a cactus, clutching a serpent. According to the legend, they would build a city in this place. From there they would be destined to rule all of Mexico. In 1325, the Aztec saw this vision on the island in Lake Texcoco. It was on this site that they founded the city of Tenochtitlán.

MAKE INFERENCES Look back at paragraph 2. What can you infer about the Aztec from the relationships they had with their neighbors?

_____

_____

_____

SUMMARIZE In one or two sentences, describe how the Aztec arrived on the island in Lake Texcoco.

_____

_____

_____

The Growth of Tenochtitlán

Tenochtitlán's beginnings were modest. Early settlers there lived in reed huts. They built floating islands on which they raised crops. Eventually, the reed huts were replaced by stone houses. A grid of streets and canals took shape. The city was divided into four main districts. From above, Tenochtitlán would have looked like a checkerboard. Over the decades, the island's swampy marshland was transformed into a grand city.

5 A group of Aztec founded another city on the island in the 1350s. As these two cities grew, they blended into one continuous urban area. Commoners throughout the island lived in neighborhoods called *calpultin* (cahl-POOL-teen). Each neighborhood was home to between ten and twenty families who shared plots of land on which they raised crops. These neighborhoods also had their own markets and temples. Local officials governed over these neighborhoods and collected tax payments from the families there.

In 1372, the tribal chief Acamapichtli was first to assume the title of *tlatoani*, or king. Under King Acamapichtli, a large pyramid with two temples was constructed in the city's center. This was known as the Great Temple. Later rulers would enlarge this tremendous structure even further. More than fifty important buildings were built around the Great Temple. These included shrines, temples, and religious schools. This area, known as the Sacred Precinct, would become the religious center of the entire Aztec Empire.

The Great Temple's pyramid towered over the city and appeared to rise out of the water to visitors approaching Tenochtitlán.

COMPARE TEXTS
Recall what you read about the construction of Tenochtitlán in the first article. How does the description on this page of the city's growth differ from what you read earlier?

_____

_____

_____

AUTHOR'S POINT OF VIEW Is the author of this article trying to inform the reader of facts or to convince the reader to accept the author's point of view?

_____

_____

_____

PARAPHRASE How would you paraphrase the first sentence of paragraph 4?

_____

_____

_____

CHRONOLOGICAL ORDER Did the city of Tenochtitlán merge with Tlatelolco before or after the Aztec joined the Triple Alliance?

_____

_____

_____

READING CHARTS How much larger was Tenochtitlán's population than London's population in 1519?

_____

_____

COMPARE AND CONTRAST POINTS OF VIEW Reread paragraph 9 on this page and paragraph 3 of "Tenochtitlán: Life in the Aztec Capital." What do these two paragraphs have in common? In what way do the two authors' points of view differ?

_____

_____

_____

The Birth of the Aztec Empire

In the late 1300s, the Aztec began forming alliances with neighboring groups. This helped them to increase their power. Many groups preferred joining forces with the Aztec to joining forces with the powerful Tepanec and Colhua people. In the late 1420s, Tenochtitlán developed an alliance with the cities Tlacopan and Texcoco. These groups formed what is known as the Triple Alliance. Together, they defeated the ruling Tepanec. This victory marked the official beginning of the Aztec Empire.

The members of the Triple Alliance were hardly equal. The Aztec continued gaining great power. They became the dominant force in the alliance. The Aztec conquered a number of other cities in the region. They soon controlled one of the largest empires in the Western Hemisphere. At its height, the Aztec Empire covered an area from the Gulf of Mexico to the Pacific Ocean. It extended south into present-day Guatemala. More than four million people lived under Aztec control.

In the 1470s, Tenochtitlán officially merged with the neighboring city of Tlatelolco. It became the largest and most densely populated city in all of Mexico and Central America. More than 200,000 people lived in an area of just five square miles. At this time, Tenochtitlán was larger than London or Seville, the finest city in Spain. The Europeans who arrived fifty years later described it as more beautiful than anything they had ever seen.

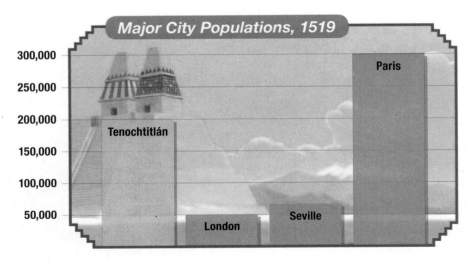

Major City Populations, 1519

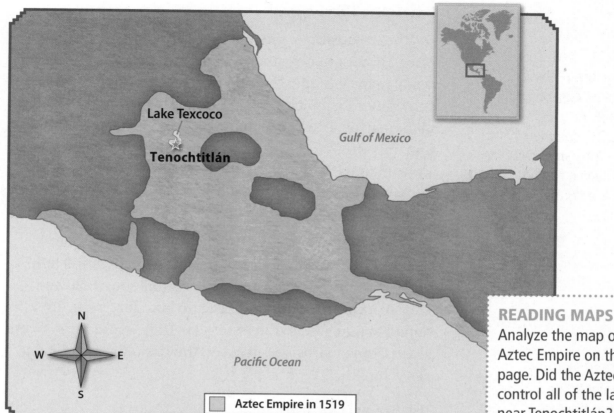

Lake Texcoco

Tenochtitlán

Gulf of Mexico

Pacific Ocean

N
W   E
S

Aztec Empire in 1519

This map shows the area controlled by the Aztec at the peak of their empire.

READING MAPS
Analyze the map of the Aztec Empire on this page. Did the Aztec fully control all of the lands near Tenochtitlán?

_____

_____

_____

Controlling the Empire

10   Throughout the late 1400s, Aztec kings expanded the empire across much of present-day Mexico. Many groups could not defend themselves against the powerful Aztec. However, Aztec kings were not very interested in governing the conquered areas far from Tenochtitlán. Instead, they wanted access to the riches available in these places. The city-states that the Aztec conquered were mostly left to govern themselves. However, these people were required to make large payments to the Aztec rulers. This is known as a tribute system. Aztec kings and nobles grew rich from the gold, cacao, and quetzal feathers acquired through these payments. The threat of further military force was enough to keep the tribute payments flowing to Tenochtitlán.

INTEGRATING INFORMATION Recall what you read in the first article about the wealth of the Aztec kings. How was this lifestyle connected to the tribute system that the Aztec imposed on the lands they conquered?

_____

_____

_____

Emerging Threats

The expansion of the Aztec Empire came with a steep price. By conquering many neighboring groups, the Aztec made many enemies. Many resented Aztec power. The Aztec sometimes forced citizens in the conquered areas to serve in their army. During the reign of King Moctezuma II, more than fifty thousand warriors rebelled against the Aztec. They were angered by the high tribute payments that the Aztec demanded. They wanted Aztec attacks on their communities to stop.

Another threat to Aztec power soon arrived in the region. In 1492, Christopher Columbus's expedition landed in the Caribbean. Spanish conquistadors soon followed. They planned to conquer and claim land for Spain. They hoped to find gold in the Americas. They wanted to convert local people to Christianity. And they would soon come to Tenochtitlán.

The Arrival of the Spanish

In 1519, the Spanish conquistador Hernán Cortés sailed from Cuba around the Yucatán Peninsula. He and about five hundred Spanish soldiers landed near present-day Veracruz, Mexico. There they met representatives of Moctezuma II. These representatives offered the Spanish exotic gifts of turquoise, jade, and gold. The Aztec hoped this would satisfy the Spanish and keep them from going any farther. They viewed the arrival of the Spanish as ominous. The Aztec had never seen such great ships as those in which the Spanish arrived. Nor had they ever seen men on horseback with metal armor. They had never before heard the roar of cannons firing.

Cortés was not satisfied by the Aztec gifts. He knew there must be far greater riches in the capital city. His expedition set off on August 16. They marched more than two hundred miles inland, over mountains and across plains. Finally, on November 8, 1519, Cortés arrived at Tenochtitlán. There he met King Moctezuma II.

GLOSSARY A glossary might give one of these meanings for expedition: *1. A journey for a purpose; 2. Promptness or speed in doing something.* Which meaning fits the way the word is used on this page?

_____

_____

_____

CONTEXT CLUES In paragraph 13, the author writes that the Aztec viewed the arrival of the Spanish as *ominous.* Underline the context clues that help you understand what this word means. Write a definition on the lines below.

_____

_____

_____

After meeting each other, Cortés and Moctezuma exchanged many valuable gifts.

15   In Tenochtitlán, Cortés and his troops were welcomed as royal guests. They were offered lavish gifts. The Spanish toured Aztec palaces, gardens, and the royal zoo. But both the Aztec and the Spanish were uneasy about each other's plans. Cortés knew that his troops were vastly outnumbered. He worried that the Aztec might attack without warning. The Aztec had heard about other native people that the Spanish had defeated. After hearing that the Aztec in Veracruz had killed some Spanish soldiers, Cortés and his troops took Moctezuma prisoner. Conflict became inevitable.

Conflict Erupts

    After Moctezuma was arrested, mayhem broke out across Tenochtitlán. Cortés tried to get Moctezuma to restore order. However, the Aztec king had lost his people's respect. He had tried to compromise with the Spanish. Many Aztec viewed this as a betrayal. Fighting grew intense. The Spanish ran short of food and water and tried to flee. Hundreds of Spanish troops were killed while trying to escape. Cortés fled over the mountains and east to the city of Tlaxcala.

    The Aztec believed that the Spanish were gone permanently. A new Aztec king took power. However, many Aztec began to get sick from a mysterious illness. The Spanish had brought smallpox with them from Europe. The Aztec had no immunity against this disease, and many died from it in the fall of 1520.

SUPPORTING DETAILS
You have read that one of the goals of the Spanish conquistadors was to find gold in the Americas. What details support this idea?

_____

_____

_____

MAIN IDEA AND SUPPORTING DETAILS
What is the main idea of paragraph 16? Write this main idea on the lines below. Circle three details in the text that support this main idea.

_____

_____

_____

COMPARE AND CONTRAST Underline the words that describe the advantages the Spanish had in the final battle for control of Tenochtitlán. Circle the words that describe the disadvantages of the Aztec. On the lines below, describe one challenge that both groups faced during the battle for Tenochtitlán.

_____

_____

_____

The Fall of Tenochtitlán

After escaping to Tlaxcala, Cortés rebuilt his army. Many local enemies of the Aztec joined him. Additional Spanish soldiers came from Cuba. Cortés's army returned to Tenochtitlán near the end of 1520. They carried enormous ships in pieces and rebuilt them on Lake Texcoco. They took control of all three of the city's causeways. The Spanish prevented food or water from reaching the Aztec on the island.

Finally, a battle began in the streets of Tenochtitlán. For months, the Aztec struggled to retain control of the city. The Spanish benefitted from their metal armor, steel swords, horses, and cannons. The Aztec were weakened by disease and hunger. The Spanish destroyed many of the city's temples and palaces. On August 13, 1521, the new Aztec king was taken prisoner. The Spanish finally controlled Tenochtitlán. The Aztec Empire had fallen.

Founding Mexico City

20   After taking control of Tenochtitlán, Spanish rulers ordered that all Aztec temples be destroyed. They filled in the city's canals with the wreckage. The lakes that surrounded the city were drained. In place of the Aztec capital, the Spanish established a new settlement. It was named Mexico City, after the Mexica people who had founded Tenochtitlán. This became the capital of the Spanish colony of New Spain for three hundred years.

Aztec Time Line

1100s	1299	1325
Aztec move into Valley of Mexico	Aztec arrive at Chapultepec Hill	Tenochtitlán founded

The Disappearance of the Aztec

After the fall of Tenochtitlán, the Aztec and other native groups continued to suffer. European diseases, including smallpox and measles, devastated the population. When Cortés arrived, central Mexico's population was about 25 million people. Within eighty years, only one million people remained.

The Aztec fought fiercely before finally being conquered by the Spanish and their allies.

READING TIME LINES
Time lines help readers keep track of when events occurred. How long after Tenochtitlán was founded did Moctezuma II take power?

On the time line, place a dot and label to show when Cortés arrived.

1375

Acamapichtli becomes first Aztec king

1420s

Triple Alliance forms, Aztec Empire begins

1502

Moctezuma II takes power

MAKE INFERENCES
Discovering the lost ruins of Tenochtitlán has been very important to the Mexican people. What evidence in the text supports this idea?

_____

_____

_____

COMPARE TEXTS
Recall what you read about the Aztec legacy in the last paragraph of the first article. How is the discussion of the cultural impact of the Aztec in this article different from the discussion in the first article?

_____

_____

_____

Rediscovering Aztec Culture

For centuries, much of the evidence of the ancient city of Tenochtitlán was lost. The Spanish wanted to eliminate any trace of the Aztec religion. They tried to convert the native people to Christianity. They built churches and missions on top of the Aztec ruins.

In 1790, workers in Mexico City made an amazing discovery. They unearthed an enormous, 25-ton Aztec altar. This was called the Sun Stone. In the nineteenth century, the Mexican government ordered that the Sun Stone be placed in the national Museum of Archaeology and History. Having declared their independence from Spain in 1810, many Mexicans wanted to rediscover the Aztec roots that formed part of their cultural heritage. Discoveries have continued ever since. In the 1970s, the ruins of the Great Temple were discovered in downtown Mexico City. The government tore down many Spanish buildings to search for the Aztec ruins underneath. The search for Aztec artifacts continues today as modern Mexico seeks to rediscover its ancient roots.

In the 1970s, the Mexican government decided to demolish a full city block and excavate the ruins of the Great Temple.

Anchor Standard Discussion Questions

Discuss the following questions with your peer group. Then record your answers in the space provided.

1. The author of "The Rise and Fall of Tenochtitlán" claims that the Spanish wanted to eliminate the Aztec religion. Do you think the author supports this statement with sufficient evidence? Why or why not?

    _____

    _____

    _____

    _____

    _____

    _____

2. Each of the two articles approaches the subject of Tenochtitlán from a different angle. Compare and contrast these two approaches. Is one approach more sympathetic toward the Aztec? Support your answer with details from both texts.

    _____

    _____

    _____

    _____

    _____

    _____

Comprehension Check

1. Why do you think building Tenochtitlán on an island helped the early Aztec to protect themselves?

_____

_____

_____

2. What was the Aztec people's goal when conquering neighboring city-states?

_____

_____

_____

3. Suppose that the Spanish had not wanted to conquer Tenochtitlán. Would their arrival still have affected Aztec life?

_____

_____

_____

Read On Your Own

Read another historical nonfiction text, "Machu Picchu," independently. Apply what you learned in this lesson and check your understanding.

Writing Informative/ Explanatory Texts

The woolly mammoth has fascinated scientists for centuries. These giant mammals lived across Europe, North America, and Siberia 10,000 to 250,000 years ago. Their physical characteristics and behavior were similar to those of modern-day elephants. About 10,000 years ago, the woolly mammoth suddenly died out, and no one knows why. If you study the woolly mammoth, how can you share the information you discover with an audience? One good way to share information is by writing an informative/explanatory text.

ESSENTIAL QUESTION

How does an informative/ explanatory text convey information?

What's an Informative/Explanatory Text?

Mammoths had shaggy hair up to three feet long that made them well adapted to colder climates. They also had giant, curved tusks that they used to protect themselves against predators, such as saber-toothed tigers and packs of hyenas. These are all facts and details that you would find in an informative/explanatory text on the woolly mammoth.

In an **informative/explanatory text**, you present information about a specific subject. The information is presented in a clear, logical way for the reader. The flow chart below describes some ways to make your informative/explanatory text effective.

Introduction
The introduction tells your reader what you are writing about. The introduction is interesting, grabs the reader's attention, and states the topic.

Body
The body includes details that support the topic. It provides facts about your topic that answer the questions *Who? What? When? Where? Why?* and *How?* It includes explanations, details, and facts.

Conclusion
The conclusion sums up your text and gives the reader something to think about.

Let's look at an informative/explanatory text.

Analyze a Mentor Text

This is an example of a fifth-grade informative/explanatory text. Read it and then complete the activities in the boxes as a class.

The Woolly Mammoth

The woolly mammoth was a huge elephant-like animal that lived in Europe, North America, and Siberia 10,000 to 250,000 years ago. It had shaggy fur and thick layers of fat to keep it warm in the frigid climate. It weighed six tons and towered almost eleven feet high. That makes the mammoth one of the largest mammals to ever walk the earth. Scientists have learned about woolly mammoths by studying their fossils and skeletons. They have learned about the size of mammoths, what they ate, and when they died out.

Everything about the mammoth was gigantic. Its large teeth were shaped like bricks and weighed ten pounds each. The trunk was six feet long. The curved tusks were also impressive. They grew up to thirteen feet long and could weigh almost 200 pounds! With such large bodies and tusks, woolly mammoths were not in danger from many predators. The only predators that threatened adult mammoths were sabertooth cats and later, humans.

Mammoths had to eat all day long to maintain their size. They were herbivores, or vegetarians, and they ate grasses, plants, tree buds, and bark. They lived on vast flat areas called steppes. The steppes were windy, dry landscapes covered with short grasses, a few trees, rivers, and streams. Other herbivores such as reindeer, musk oxen, and horses also lived on the steppes. Mammoths used their trunks to reach down and tear out grass. Scientists believe they used their tusks to scrape the ground and dig up plants or rip off tree bark.

TOPIC The writer gets the reader's attention in the introduction by describing the woolly mammoth's huge size. The writer also states the topic—the woolly mammoth—and tells the main idea. Draw a box around the topic sentence that states the main idea.

SUPPORTING DETAILS In the second and third paragraphs, the writer gives details that support the main idea, and explanations and facts that elaborate on the details. In each paragraph, put a box around the strong supporting detail. Underline the explanations and facts that elaborate on the supporting detail.

SUPPORTING DETAILS
In the fourth paragraph, the writer provides one more strong detail that supports the main idea of the text, along with explanations and facts that elaborate on the supporting detail. Draw a box around the strong supporting detail, and underline the sentences that elaborate on the detail with explanations and facts.

CONCLUSION In the conclusion, the writer sums up the informative text and gives the reader something to think about. Draw a star by the sentence that gives you something to think about.

The woolly mammoth died out about 10,000 years ago. Scientists are not sure why it became extinct. Some scientists believe that a massive climate change caused the world to grow warmer and the glaciers to melt. As oceans rose, the mammoth's habitat disappeared. Therefore, the mammoth had a difficult time finding food. Another theory suggests that humans may have hunted the mammoth to extinction. Whatever the cause, the woolly mammoth disappeared from most of its territory at the end of the last ice age.

Scientists have studied mammoths for a long time and learned a lot about them. However, we still have a lot to learn about these magnificent creatures. By studying fossils and bones, maybe someday we will learn why the woolly mammoth disappeared.

Think About It ▶ Why do you think the author chose to write about the woolly mammoth?

What part of the informative/explanatory text did you find most interesting? Why?

Vocabulary Study: Using Glossaries and Dictionaries

A **glossary** and a **dictionary** are similar. Glossaries and dictionaries are both alphabetical lists of words that tell you what a word means, how to say the word, and sometimes where the word comes from. A glossary is found at the back of some books and gives information on important words used in the book. A dictionary is a book or online resource that includes most of the words used in the English language. Work with your class or a partner to answer the questions below.

mam • moth /**mam ′əth**/ [from the Russian *mamont, mamot*] *noun* 1. a type of large extinct mammal of the elephant family that lived long ago, distinguished from the modern elephant by its shaggy fur and long, curved tusks. *adjective* 2. very big; huge; gigantic.

1. How many syllables are in the word *mammoth?*

   _____

2. How many definitions are given?

   _____

3. Write a sentence using the word *mammoth* as an adjective.

   _____

   _____

bark /**bärk**/ [Middle English *berken,* from Old English *beorcan;* similar to Old Norse *berkja* to bark] *noun* 1. tough outside covering of the trunk and branches of a tree. *noun* 2. the sharp sound made by a dog. *verb* 3. to scrape the skin by bumping into something. *verb* 4. to speak in a loud, usually angry tone.

Answer the following questions on your own.

4. How many syllables are in the word *bark?*

   _____

5. How many definitions are given?

   _____

6. Write a sentence using the fourth definition of *bark*.

   _____

   _____

Writing Process

Now that you have read and analyzed an informative/explanatory text, you are going to create your own by following these steps of the writing process.

1. Get Ready: Take Notes on Research Use reliable sources of information to research a topic and take notes. Research visual information about a topic and take notes.

2. Organize Use a graphic organizer to organize your notes and plan your informative/explanatory text.

3. Draft Create the first draft of your informative/explanatory text.

4. Peer Review Work with a partner to evaluate and improve your draft.

5. Revise Use suggestions from your peer review to revise your draft.

6. Edit Check your work carefully for spelling, punctuation, and grammar errors.

7. Publish Create a final version of your informative/explanatory text.

Writing Assignment

In this lesson, you will write your own informative/explanatory text. As you create this piece, remember the elements of the mentor text that were most effective. Read the following assignment.

Write an informative/explanatory text about the yeti crab, a new species that has been discovered in recent years. Describe what this animal looks like, where it was discovered, and how it is unusual or different.

1. Get Ready: Take Notes on Research

The writer of the mentor text wrote about the woolly mammoth. Before she could write a draft, she researched her topic. Here is a paragraph from a journal she found in the library.

March 28th, 2001 — Siberia

On Monday we began digging through the frozen ground of the Siberian tundra. The tusks curled up from the frozen ground like the ribs of a giant beast. It took the team three days to chop through the ground surrounding the tusks. After the extraction, we transported the tusks by helicopter to a laboratory.

The tusks measured nine and a half feet long. They weighed more than one hundred pounds. Based on this analysis, we concluded that they came from a mammoth eleven feet tall.

The writer took notes on each of the books she found. Here is the note card that she filled out for the text above. What kinds of information does she include?

Main Idea: Scientists found the tusks of a woolly mammoth in Siberia.

Detail: The woolly mammoth tusks were nine and a half feet long.

Detail: The woolly mammoth tusks weighed more than a hundred pounds.

Detail: Based on the analysis, the woolly mammoth was eleven feet tall.

Source: Aydeb, James V. "Excavating Mammoths." *Deepdown* (2003): 76–78.

MAIN IDEA On the first line, she wrote an important idea from the passage that she was interested in using in her report.

DETAILS She next listed details from the passage. How do the details support the main idea?

SOURCE Finally, she wrote where she found the passage. Where did she find this passage?

Researching Text

Your topic is the yeti crab. Here is some information from a newspaper article that you might use in your informative piece. Read the text. Think about the important ideas in each paragraph and how the details support the main ideas. Also think about which details are relevant to the topic of your informative piece, and whether any of the details are not relevant.

MAIN IDEA What do you think is the most important idea in the first paragraph?

DETAILS Which explanations, details, or facts would best support the ideas in your informative/ explanatory text? Are any details not important for your topic?

DETAILS This paragraph compares and contrasts the yeti crabs found in the Pacific with those in Antarctica. Which details would best support the main ideas of your paper?

Yeti Crab Found!

By Bryan Michael Block

Scientists exploring deep under the surface of the ocean near Antarctica made a startling discovery today—a previously unseen species of the yeti crab. These hairy-chested crabs were found gathered near a hydrothermal vent miles under the ocean's surface. Hydrothermal vents are caused by underwater volcanoes that shoot up hot water that can reach more than 750 degrees Fahrenheit. Many kinds of organisms live in the warm waters near the vents. Some hydrothermal vents form chimney-shaped structures as high as 60 meters. Scientists were startled to find almost 600 yeti crabs living in a small area around a vent near an area called the East Scotia Ridge.

Kiwa hirsuta, the first known yeti crab, was found living near a hydrothermal vent in the South Pacific in 2005. However, *Kiwa hirsuta* and the yeti crabs found today are slightly different. Both crabs have long hair on their claws and limbs. The yeti crabs in Antarctica, however, have a dense pad of hair on their undersides, or chests. In addition, the number of crabs found in the South Pacific was much smaller than the number of crabs found near Antarctica.

Source: Block, Bryan Michael. "Yeti Crab Found!" *The Owl News* [Chicago] 3 Jan. 2012: 2–3.

Try It!

Record Your Notes

Use these note cards to take notes on the text about yeti crabs. Remember, write the main idea and supporting details of each paragraph. Finally, give the source of the information.

Main Idea:
Detail:
Detail:
Detail:
Source:

Main Idea:
Detail:
Detail:
Detail:
Source:

Researching Visual Information

When you research a topic, you will discover that information can be given in different ways. You may find pictures or photographs in online resources. You may find information given in diagrams and maps. You can use note cards to record your notes about these different forms of information, too.

The first example shows a picture of the yeti crab. The second example shows a map. Think about how you could use both to gather details about the yeti crab.

INFORMATION IN PICTURES How could you use the information shown in the picture to help you describe the yeti crab to your audience?

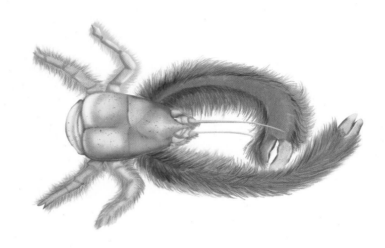

INFORMATION IN GRAPHIC FEATURES How could this map help you write an informative text about yeti crabs? What information would you use?

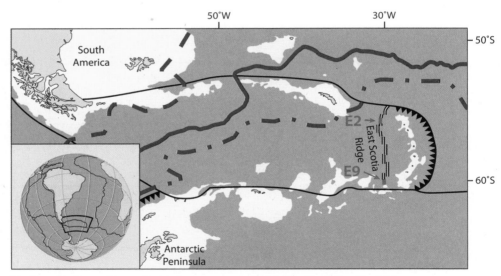

Yeti crabs have been found near vent E9 in the East Scotia Ridge on the ocean floor.

Source: Block, Bryan Michael. "Yeti Crab Found!"
The Owl News [Chicago] 3 Jan. 2012: 2–3.

Try It!

Record Your Notes

Use these note cards to take notes on the picture and map shown on the previous page. You can use your answers from the activities on that page to help you.

Main Idea (Picture):
Detail:
Detail:
Detail:
Source:

Main Idea (Map):
Detail:
Detail:
Detail:
Source:

2. Organize

You are almost ready to begin a draft of your informative/explanatory text. You can use a graphic organizer to help organize the ideas and details. You can then refer to the graphic organizer as you work through the different parts of your draft. The writer of the mentor text completed this graphic organizer.

INTRODUCTION In the first paragraph, you

- tell the topic and main idea of your informative/explanatory text.

SUPPORTING PARAGRAPHS In the second, third, and fourth paragraphs, you

- give three strong details that support the main idea
- elaborate on the details with explanations and facts

CONCLUSION Your conclusion should

- briefly summarize your text
- give the reader something to think about

Main Idea
Scientists have learned about the size of mammoths, what they ate, and when they died out.

Supporting Detail 1
Everything about the mammoth was gigantic, including the teeth, trunk, and tusks.

Supporting Detail 2
Mammoths were herbivores, or vegetarians. They ate only plants. They lived on the steppes, where it was very cold.

Supporting Detail 3
Mammoths died out around 10,000 years ago. There are various theories about why they became extinct.

Conclusion
Scientists have learned a great deal from studying mammoth fossils and bones. Maybe someday we can learn why the woolly mammoth disappeared.

Try It!

Organize Your Informative/Explanatory Text

Now use the graphic organizer below to organize the ideas and details you want to use in the different paragraphs of your draft.

Main Idea

Supporting Detail 1

Supporting Detail 2

Supporting Detail 3

Conclusion

3. Draft

Now it is time to begin the first draft of your informative/explanatory text. Remember, your draft does not have to be perfect! This is the time to use your notes, get your ideas down in some sort of organized way, and have fun. You will have time to revise your writing later. Start by drafting your informative/explanatory text on a computer or on a separate sheet of paper. Tell about the yeti crab, a new species that has been discovered in recent years.

Writer's Craft: Using Linking Words and Phrases

Linking words and phrases help writing flow smoothly. They also help readers understand how ideas are linked within and across categories. Here are some common linking words and phrases.

Linking words	*also, although, additionally, and, another, because, before, especially, first, finally, however, more, surpisingly, then, therefore, whatever*
Linking phrases	*for example, even though, in addition, in contrast, one reason, as a result, exploring further*

The author of the mentor text uses linking words and phrases in the fourth paragraph.

LINKING WORDS AND PHRASES
Read this section of the mentor text. Circle the linking words and phrases that connect ideas.

The woolly mammoth died out about 10,000 years ago. Scientists are not sure why it became extinct. Some scientists believe that a massive climate change caused the world to grow warmer and the glaciers to melt. As oceans rose, the mammoth's habitat disappeared. Therefore, the mammoth had a difficult time finding food. Another theory suggests that humans may have hunted the mammoth to extinction. Whatever the cause, the woolly mammoth disappeared from most of its territory at the end of the last ice age.

Try It!   **Write Your First Draft**

On a computer or a separate sheet of paper, create the draft of your response to the writing assignment. Remember to use linking words in your writing. Use this drafting checklist to help you as you write.

✔ A good beginning gets your reader's attention. You can begin with a question, a quotation, or an interesting fact about your species.

✔ Be sure to state your main idea in a clear topic sentence in the first paragraph.

✔ Be sure every paragraph includes a strong supporting detail for the topic, as well as explanations and facts that elaborate on the detail.

✔ Use the details you wrote during Step 2: Organize.

✔ Illustrate your text with visuals, such as photographs, maps, or graphics.

✔ Try to write a conclusion that is satisfying, sums up your paper in a memorable way, and leaves the reader with something to think about.

Tips for Writing Your First Draft

- As you start writing, make sure to use your graphic organizer to plan your paragraphs.

- Focus on ideas, not details. Since you will revise and edit later, you can fix the details then. In drafting, it's the ideas that count.

- Sometimes students write better after physical activity. If you get stuck, take a break, stand up, and do a few stretches. Then try again!

4. Peer Review

After you finish your draft, you will work with a partner to review each other's drafts. Here is a draft of the mentor text. Read it with your partner. Together, answer the questions in the boxes. Then we'll see how the writer's classmate evaluated the draft.

An Early Draft:

INTRODUCTION In her draft, the writer does not include a clear main idea. What is the main idea of the text?

SUPPORTING PARAGRAPHS The third paragraph talks about Asian elephants. Does this information support the main idea?

CONCLUSION The conclusion does not really summarize the main idea of the text. How could the main idea be better summed up?

The Woolly Mammoth

The woolly mammoth was a huge animal that lived in Europe, North America, and Siberia 10,000 to 250,000 years ago. It had shaggy fur and thick layers of fat. It weighed six tons and towered almost eleven feet high. That makes the mammoth one of the largest mammals to ever walk the earth.

Everything about the mammoth was gigantic. Its molars were shaped like bricks and weighed ten pounds each. The trunk was six feet long. The tusks were also impressive. They twisted and curved and could grow up to thirteen feet long. Scientists have found tusks that weigh almost 200 pounds. Adult woolly mammoths were not in danger from many predators.

Mammoths needed to eat all day long to maintain their size. Mammoths were herbivores, or vegetarians. Their diet consisted of grasses, plants, tree buds, and bark. Scientists think mammoths used their tusks to dig up plants, or rip off tree bark. The Asian elephant resembles the woolly mammoth. It has tusks like a mammoth, but they are shorter and curve only slightly. They also like to eat grass and sugarcane. Asian elephants live in Southeast Asia.

The woolly mammoth died out 10,000 years ago. As oceans rose, the mammoth's habitat disappeared. Therefore, the mammoth had a difficult time finding food. The mammoths died out in great numbers 10,000 years ago.

Scientists have studied mammoths for a long time. Maybe they will learn why the woolly mammoth disappeared.

An Example Peer Review Form

This peer review form gives an example of how a classmate evaluated the draft of the mentor text shown on the previous page.

The introduction states the topic in an interesting way.	You did a good job of *getting the reader's attention.*
The main idea of the text is clear.	You could improve your informative/explanatory text by *including a main idea.*

The writer supports the main idea with at least three strong supporting details.	You did a good job of *giving three supporting details.*
The writer includes explanations, details, and facts.	You could improve your informative/explanatory text by *deleting facts that do not support the main idea and adding more explanations and facts to the supporting paragraphs.*

The writer uses linking words and phrases correctly.	You did a good job of *using "therefore" in the fourth paragraph.*
	You could improve your informative/explanatory text by *using more linking words and phrases to connect ideas.*

The writer includes a satisfying conclusion.	You did a good job of *including a concluding paragraph and giving the reader something to think about.*
The conclusion sums up the text and gives the reader something to think about.	You could improve your informative/explanatory text by *adding one or two sentences that briefly sum up your text.*

Try It! Peer Review with a Partner

Now you are going to work with a partner to review each other's drafts. You will use the peer review form below. If you need help, look back at the mentor text writer's peer review form for suggestions.

The introduction states the topic in an interesting way. **The main idea of the paper is clear.**	You did a good job of
	You could improve your draft by

The writer supports the main idea with at least three strong supporting details. **The writer includes explanations, details, and facts.**	You did a good job of
	You could improve your draft by

The writer uses linking words and phrases correctly.	You did a good job of
	You could improve your draft by

The writer includes a satisfying conclusion. **The conclusion sums up the paper and gives the reader something to think about.**	You did a good job of
	You could improve your draft by

Try It!   **Record Key Peer Review Comments**

Now it's time for you and your partner to share your comments with each other.
Listen to your partner's feedback, and write down the key comments in the left
column. Then write some ideas for improving your draft in the right column.

My review says that my introduction	I will
My review says that my supporting details	I will
My review says that my use of details and explanations	I will
My review says that my use of linking words	I will
My review says that my conclusion	I will

Use the space below to write anything else that you notice about your draft
that you think you can improve.

5. Revise

In this step of the writing process, you will work on parts of your draft that need improvement. Use the peer review form that your classmate completed to help you. Also use your own ideas about how to improve each part of your draft. This checklist includes some things to think about as you get ready to revise.

Revision Checklist

✓ Does my beginning catch the reader's interest? Do I state my main idea clearly?

✓ Do I support my main idea with at least three strong supporting details?

✓ Do I use explanations and facts to elaborate on the supporting details?

✓ Does my conclusion sum up the paper well? Have I given the reader something to think about?

✓ Do I use linking words and phrases effectively to make the writing flow smoothly?

✓ Do I use precise language to make my ideas as clear and vivid as they can be?

PRECISE LANGUAGE
Precise language means words or phrases that are clear, specific, and descriptive. Underline precise language in this paragraph.

Look at the word *animal* in the first sentence. Would *mammal* have been more or less precise in this sentence? Why?

_____

_____

Writer's Craft: Using Precise Language

Using precise words makes your informative/explanatory text clearer and more convincing. For example, instead of using the word *kind*, you might use the more precise word *sympathetic*. Instead of the word *dog*, you might say *golden retriever*. Now look at the mentor text for examples of precise language.

The woolly mammoth was a huge elephant-like animal that lived in Europe, North America, and Siberia 10,000 to 250,000 years ago. It had shaggy fur and thick layers of fat to keep it warm in the frigid climate. It weighed six tons and towered almost eleven feet high.

Try It!

Revise Your Informative/Explanatory Text

Replacing simple words with more descriptive or precise words is an important part of revising. Practice using precise language with the following paragraph. Replace each underlined word with a more precise, more interesting word. Write your answers on the lines below the paragraph.

> Scientists take special precautions when studying mammoth bones. First, they use small brushes to <u>take away</u> any dust and dirt. Then they <u>look at</u> each bone very carefully with a magnifying glass or microscope. The bones are then <u>put</u> in a dry environment where the temperature <u>is</u> the same all the time.

Replace *take away* with _____

Replace *look at* with _____

Replace *put* with _____

Replace *is* with _____

Writing Assignment

Now it's time to revise the draft of your informative/explanatory text. Continue working on a computer or on a separate sheet of paper. Review the assignment, repeated below, and the checklist. Doing so will help you know that you have included everything you need.

> Write an informative/explanatory text about the yeti crab, a new species that has been discovered in recent years. Describe what this animal looks like, where it was discovered, and how it is unusual or different.

6. Edit

After revising your informative/explanatory text, you will edit it. When you edit, you read very carefully to be sure to find any mistakes in your writing. Here's a checklist of some things to look for as you edit.

> **Editing Checklist**
>
> ✔ Did you indent each paragraph?
>
> ✔ Are all of your sentences complete? Does each have a subject and a verb?
>
> ✔ Did you begin each sentence with a capital letter?
>
> ✔ Does each sentence end with the correct punctuation?
>
> ✔ Have you used commas correctly?
>
> ✔ Are all of your words spelled correctly?

You can use these editing marks to mark any errors you find.

^ Add	delete Delete
# Add space	⌒ Close up space

This section of a paragraph from a draft of the mentor text shows how to use editing marks.

Other herbivores such as rein deer muskoxen and horses also lived on off the steppes. Mammoths used their trunks to reach down and tear out grass. Scientists believe they used their tusks to scrap scrape the ground and dig up plants or rip off tree bark.

Language Focus: Varying Sentence Style

Varying sentence style makes your writing more interesting for the reader. Variety also makes the text read more smoothly and adds interest to your writing. There are many ways to vary sentence style in your writing.

- Combining sentences will help make your writing stronger.
  - Original: Mammoths had thick fur. The fur was shaggy.
  - Combined: Mammoths had thick, shaggy fur.

- Avoid short, choppy writing by adding details.
  - Short sentence: Scientists study mammoth bones.
  - Detailed sentence: Scientists study mammoth bones with microscopes to look for teeth marks or marks made by stone tools.

- Changing the beginnings of your sentences is a good way to add variety to your writing. Begin a sentence with an introductory word, phrase, or clause.
  - Original: The mammoth's habitat disappeared when oceans rose.
  - Changed: As oceans rose, the mammoth's habitat disappeared.

- Reduce sentences that contain unnecessary information.
  - Original: Mammoths had to eat all day long throughout the day to maintain their size.
  - Changed: Mammoths had to eat all day long to maintain their size.

Everything about the mammoth was gigantic. Its large teeth were shaped like bricks and weighed ten pounds each. The trunk was six feet long. The curved tusks were also impressive. They grew up to thirteen feet long and could weigh almost 200 pounds! With such large bodies and tusks, woolly mammoths were not in danger from many predators. The only predators that threatened adult mammoths were sabertooth cats and later, humans.

VARYING SENTENCE STYLE Read this section of the mentor text. Use the information on this page to underline sentences that combine more than one idea or fact. Place a square around the sentence that begins with an introductory phrase.

Try It! Language and Editing Practice

Combine the following sentences.

1. My dog sleeps on my bed. My dog wakes me up early.

   _____

2. Mr. Patrick lives down the street. Mr. Patrick is the mayor.

   _____

Add details to the following sentences.

3. I looked for my shoes.

   _____

4. We walked upstairs.

   _____

Reduce the following sentences to eliminate unnecessary information.

5. Mammoth bones are carefully cleaned, and they are cleaned using soft brushes.

   _____

6. Scientists use a magnifying glass to study the bones, and they also use a microscope to study the bones.

   _____

7. Scientists look for signs of wear, and they also look for bite marks.

   _____

Try It!

Edit Your Informative/Explanatory Text

Now edit your informative/explanatory text. Use this checklist and the editing marks you have learned to correct any errors you find.

☐ Do the subjects and verbs in your sentences agree?

☐ Are there any missing or repeated words in your sentences?

☐ Have you followed the rules of capitalization?

☐ Have you added variety to your sentences by combining sentences, adding details, starting your sentences in different ways, and reducing sentences that contain unnecessary information?

☐ Have you followed the rules of punctuation?

Editing Tips

- Write down key phrases and ideas before you begin writing. Sometimes this is a great warm-up to get you started!

- Listen carefully as you read your work aloud. Do you need to take a breath when you're reading some of the sentences? That might indicate sentences that are run-ons.

- Use your finger or a pencil to point at each word as you read it. This will help you slow down and find easy-to-miss mistakes.

7. Publish

On a computer or a separate sheet of paper, create a neat final draft of your informative/explanatory text.

Correct all errors that you identified while editing your draft. Be sure to give your informative/explanatory text an interesting title.

The final step is to publish your informative/explanatory text. Here are some different ways you might choose to share your work.

- Read your informative/explanatory text aloud to your class or to a small group of your classmates.

- Create a class book or magazine that includes all the texts about the yeti crab, as well as pictures or diagrams.

- Create a poster, using your informative/explanatory text and drawings or photographs from magazines or newspapers.

- Display your informative/explanatory text on the class bulletin board.

Technology Suggestions

- **Publish your informative/explanatory text in a multimedia presentation using digital images and photographs.**
- **Create a simple Web page about the new species of yeti crab.**

Reading Technical Texts

Look at this person giving a presentation. How do graphics help an audience understand information?

ESSENTIAL QUESTION

What are some ways that technical texts present information?

What tools do meteorologists use to predict the weather?

What can scientists learn about weather by using technology?

How a Meteorologist Predicts the Weather

TECHNICAL TEXTS

Technical texts explain how to do something or how something works. They are usually about science, math, or technology. Technical texts often use subheads, diagrams, photographs, tables, and illustrations to give information to the reader. What is explained in this selection?

CONTEXT CLUES Context clues are words near an unknown word that give clues to its meaning. If you don't know the meaning of a certain word, you can look at the words around it to figure out its meaning. Look at the word *meteorologist* in paragraph 4. What context clues let you know what this word means?

1   When you wake up in the morning, do you look out the window to check the weather? The daily conditions of the atmosphere affect everything from how we dress in the morning to the events we plan for the day. Many people, such as farmers and pilots, need information about these conditions in order to do their jobs. They rely on meteorologists to make predictions about the weather.

Throughout the centuries, people have observed the sky and tried to predict if the next day would bring sunshine, rain, or snow. Sometimes people made up rhymes to help them remember certain clues:

> *Red sky at night, sailors' delight.*
> *Red sky in morning, sailors take warning.*

Although using rhymes such as this might sound unscientific, sometimes these traditional rhymes can be accurate. In some areas of the world, if the sky is red at night, it means clouds are parting in the west, and the next day will probably bring clear weather. If the clouds are red in the morning, it means low clouds are moving in, and there is a likelihood of rain or storms.

Today, meteorologists use more advanced technology to forecast the weather. They take measurements from thousands of land-based weather stations located around the world. Meteorologists study the information from these instruments to make short-range forecasts for the next twenty-four hours. They can also make longer-range forecasts, although these are less reliable. No single tool gives meteorologists a complete picture of the weather. They must gather information from many sources to make an inference about what the weather will be.

Meteorologists analyze information from many sources to forecast the weather.

Weather Stations

5   About ten thousand stations around the world gather information about weather. Weather stations use various instruments to measure temperature, air pressure, humidity, wind speed, and other conditions. The stations are located in deserts, mountains, cities, rain forests, and oceans. There is even a station in Antarctica! Four times a day, each station sends information to meteorological centers in Australia, Russia, and the United States. These centers then distribute the information to meteorologists around the world.

Common Weather Station Instruments

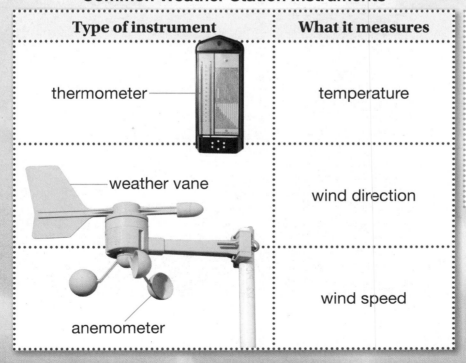

Type of instrument	What it measures
thermometer	temperature
weather vane	wind direction
anemometer	wind speed

CHARTS A chart organizes information visually. Charts enable readers to quickly and easily identify important pieces of information. Look at the chart of weather station instruments. How does the chart help you understand what a weather station does?

Weather Radar

Radar is one of a meteorologist's most valuable tools. The term *radar* is short for "radio detection and ranging." Radar works by sending out radio waves to sweep across the sky. These waves reflect off objects in the sky, similar to the way visible light reflects off objects. The reflection returns to the radar station. Depending on the condition of the returning reflection, meteorologists can determine whether the outgoing waves encountered rain, snow, or hail.

Weather radar has two parts. The transmitter sends out the radio waves into the air. When the waves hit rain, snow, or hail, they reflect, or echo, back. The second part, the receiver, is the part of the radar that picks up the echo.

Meteorologists use radar to track and study storms, hurricanes, and tornadoes. Using this tool, meteorologists can estimate, or make a good guess about, the size of a storm, the direction in which it is heading, and how dangerous it is.

CONTEXT CLUES Look at the word *estimate* in paragraph 8. What context clues help you figure out what this word means?

Meteorologists use radar to study storms.

Satellites

Radar is important in forecasting weather a day in advance, but it cannot provide a long-range forecast. Weather satellites, on the other hand, can help meteorologists predict conditions days or even a week in advance. These satellites are recording stations that are launched into space. They orbit, or circle the globe, high above Earth. From there, they take pictures of the weather below. Meteorologists study the satellite images to follow the movement of clouds, as well as wind speed and storms. For example, satellites can indicate the size and speed of tropical storms and hurricanes that form far out in the ocean. By studying satellite images, meteorologists can predict where these storms might hit land.

Weather satellites like this one orbit high above Earth, sending back images of cloud formations and other weather conditions.

Weather Balloons

10   Every day, at noon and midnight, hundreds of meteorologists around the world release gas-filled weather balloons into the sky. Each balloon is about 6 feet across and carries a radiosonde, an instrument that measures temperature, air pressure, and humidity. The balloon gradually ascends to a height of about 35,000 meters, or 20 miles, above Earth. As the balloon rises, the radiosonde sends its measurements by radio to a weather station located on the ground. When the balloon reaches a high enough height, it explodes. The radiosonde then falls back to Earth on a small parachute. The radiosonde has a mailing bag attached. If someone finds it, it can be returned by mail and used again.

CONTEXT CLUES Look at the word *ascends* in paragraph 10. What context clues can help you figure out what this word means?

CHRONOLOGICAL ORDER Chronological order refers to the order in which things happen. Reread paragraph 10. What three things happen after meteorologists release a weather balloon into the sky?

Airplanes

Meteorologists use airplanes modified with special instruments to study weather at different altitudes. These instruments are attached to the outside of airplanes and record wind speed, temperature, and other information. The airplanes also have special radar and lasers that take three-dimensional (3-D) images of clouds. These images provide more details than the instruments attached to balloons. Meteorologists also use these airplanes to monitor hurricanes. Sometimes, they will even fly the planes into the "eye," or center, of the storm!

Some areas of a severe storm may be too dangerous for people to fly into. Meteorologists are testing robotic airplanes to help solve this problem. These small airplanes weigh anywhere from twenty to forty pounds. A pilot on the ground operates the airplane by remote control. Because it doesn't have humans on board, a robotic plane can fly into the most dangerous part of a storm without risking lives. The plane can carry instruments that measure conditions in that part of the storm. This information can help meteorologists make more accurate predictions about a storm's progress.

CONTEXT CLUES Look at the word *modified* in paragraph 11. What information does the paragraph give that can help you figure out what this word means?

DIAGRAMS Look at the diagram of the airplane used for collecting weather information. How is this airplane different from a regular airplane?

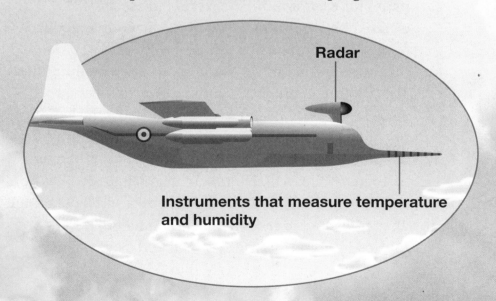

Radar

Instruments that measure temperature and humidity

Buoys

Meteorologists use buoys to gather information about conditions at sea. These buoys are floating weather stations anchored to the bottom of the ocean. Like other weather stations, buoys use instruments to measure wind, air pressure, and temperature. After collecting measurements, buoys send this information to satellites in space. The satellites then beam the information to meteorologists on land.

CHRONOLOGICAL ORDER
Reread paragraph 13. What happens after the buoys collect weather measurements?

The Future of Weather Forecasting

Thanks to science and technology, our methods for predicting the weather have grown more accurate over time. Tools such as weather stations and satellites have made forecasts more precise. As a result, many lives have been saved, and many disasters have been avoided.

Meteorologists can warn people about severe weather.

Comprehension Check

Look back at the chart on page 119 and the diagram on page 122 in "How a Meteorologist Predicts the Weather." Then use the organizer below to summarize the information given in the chart and the diagram.

Charts and Diagrams
What information do the chart and the diagram give?

Chart:

The chart shows _____

_____

_____

_____

_____

_____

_____

_____

_____

_____

_____

_____

Diagram:

The diagram shows _____

_____

_____

_____

_____

_____

_____

_____

_____

_____

_____

_____

Vocabulary

Use the word map below to help you define and use one of the highlighted vocabulary words from the Share and Learn selection you are about to read or another word you choose.

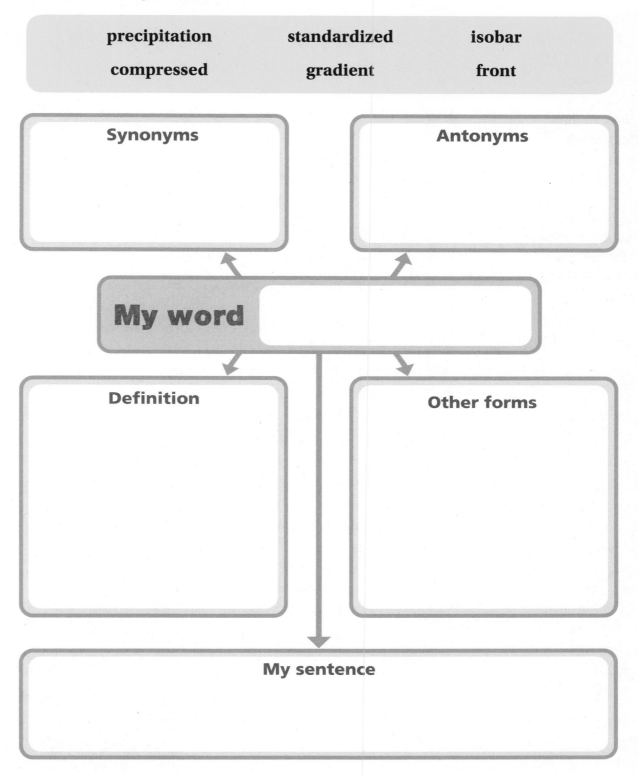

precipitation   standardized   isobar

compressed   gradient   front

Synonyms

Antonyms

My word

Definition

Other forms

My sentence

Consider ▶ What information is shown on a weather map?

Why is understanding how to read a weather map important?

Reading a Weather Map

CONTEXT CLUES What phrases in paragraph 2 help you understand the meaning of the word standardized? Circle them.

PARAPHRASE Reread paragraph 2. Paraphrase the information about how symbols are used on weather maps.

_____

_____

_____

_____

_____

CHRONOLOGICAL ORDER What must meteorologists do before they create a weather map? Which article in this lesson describes this first step that meteorologists take?

1　　Meteorologists use the information they gather to create weather maps. Some weather maps show a small area, such as a county or part of a state. Other weather maps show a larger region of the United States, the whole country, or other areas of the world. In any case, these maps show what the weather is doing at that moment in the region shown on the map. They can also tell you what kind of weather to expect in the next few hours or days.

Getting Started

　　Like road maps, weather maps include a large amount of information. They use symbols, or special markings, to indicate atmospheric conditions such as temperature, air pressure, the amount of cloud cover, precipitation, and severe storms. If these symbols are unfamiliar to you, a weather map may look complicated and confusing. It can look like a jumble of squiggly lines and numbers. However, it is not hard to learn what the symbols mean. And most weather maps use standardized symbols, so once you understand what the symbols mean, you will be able to read almost any weather map. Knowing how to read a weather map can also help you better understand weather forecasts. That's a good thing. If you want to go to the beach or spend the day at the park, it's helpful to know as much as possible about what the weather is likely to be.

The weather affects us in many ways. Why is it helpful to know what the weather is likely to be?

What to Look for First

One of the first things you should look for when reading a weather map is areas of high or low pressure. Each is marked with a large "H" for high or "L" for low. If the map is in color, the H symbols are normally in blue, and the L symbols are in red. Where you see an H, the air pressure is high, and weather in that area is usually clear and fair. Where you see an L, the pressure is low. The weather in a low-pressure area is more likely to have stronger winds, sometimes with rain or snow.

The weather map below shows high-pressure areas in western Canada, Montana, Idaho, West Virginia, and north of New York state, near Lake Ontario. It shows low-pressure areas near the coast of California and in Arizona, Oklahoma, and eastern Canada.

MAKE INFERENCES
Reread paragraph 3. Do you think storms occur in high-pressure or low-pressure areas? What information supports this inference?

_____

_____

_____

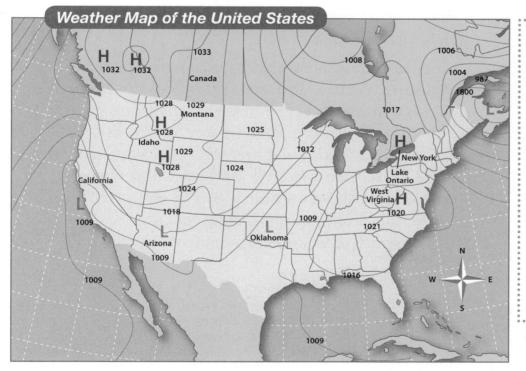

Weather Map of the United States

CITE EVIDENCE On the day represented on this map, was the air pressure in the northwestern United States mostly high or mostly low? What evidence can you cite from the map to support your answer?

_____

_____

_____

Isobars and Air Pressure

5   Next you should look for isobars. Isobars are lines on the map that show areas where the air pressure is the same. Look back at the map on page 127. Look at the high-pressure symbol in western Montana. You will see an isobar that traces an oval shape around the symbol. Next to the line is the number 1029. That tells you that the air pressure along the line is 1029 millibars. Millibars are the units of measure that meteorologists use to calculate air pressure. Normal or average air pressure at sea level is about 1013 millibars. The air pressure in Montana is about 16 millibars higher than average.

     Now look at the low-pressure symbol in Oklahoma. The symbol is near an isobar line that has the number 1009. If you trace this line westward toward California, you will see that the low-pressure area in California is near the same 1009-millibar line. All along this line, the air pressure is about 4 millibars lower than average.

     Where the pressure is higher, the air is being compressed, or squeezed, tighter than in areas of low pressure. As a result, air flows from high-pressure areas to low-pressure areas. This flowing air is what causes winds, storms, and many other weather events. The lower the pressure in a low-pressure area, the more severe the weather is likely to be. Under normal conditions, the air pressure rarely goes below 980 millibars. However, hurricanes and other dangerous tropical storms may form when pressures are lower than 900 millibars.

CONTEXT CLUES
Reread paragraph 7. Circle the details that help you understand the meaning of compressed.

DIAGRAMS Look at the diagram on this page. How does the diagram add to what the text tells you about air flowing from high-pressure to low-pressure areas?

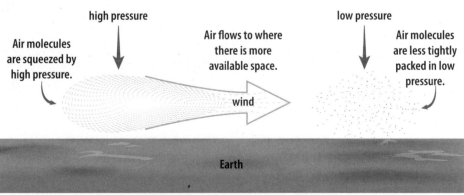

Wind is created by air flowing from a high-pressure area to a low-pressure area.

North of the equator, air flows clockwise around areas of high pressure and counterclockwise around areas of low pressure.

Wind Flow Patterns

Air flows from high-pressure to low-pressure areas, but it doesn't flow in a straight line. Instead, the winds flow in circular patterns. Think about water going down the drain of your sink. It doesn't go straight down. Instead, it circles around the drain and forms a whirlpool. Moving air behaves in a similar way. The air flowing away from a high-pressure area whirls in a clockwise direction. Air flowing around a low-pressure area circles in a counterclockwise direction. This is what happens in the northern hemisphere—the part of the earth north of the equator. In the southern hemisphere, airflows whirl in the opposite direction.

Look again at the map on page 127. Look at the high-pressure symbol in West Virginia. The air will be flowing in a clockwise circle around this area and also flowing away from it. Some of this wind will be flowing toward the low-pressure area in eastern Canada. As it approaches the low-pressure area, the wind will flow counterclockwise around it. You can also see that the isobars around the low-pressure area in eastern Canada are closer together than the isobars in other parts of the map. That means there is a steep pressure gradient, or that the pressure changes rapidly near the low-pressure area. A steep pressure gradient causes stronger winds.

PARAPHRASE
Paraphrase the information in paragraph 8 about how winds flow in circular patterns.

_____

_____

_____

CONTEXT CLUES
Circle the details in the text that help you understand the meaning of the word gradient.

Interpreting a Weather Map

10   Look at the map on the page 131. This map shows a high-pressure area in Pennsylvania. The blue arrows show the winds circling clockwise around this high-pressure area and also flowing toward a low-pressure area in Minnesota. Orange arrows show the winds circling counter-clockwise around this low-pressure area. The numbers on this map indicate the temperature in degrees Fahrenheit. It is 83 degrees Fahrenheit in central Florida. What is the temperature near Denver?

This map also shows fronts, or boundaries between masses of air. The symbols for fronts are shown in the map key. Cold fronts are indicated by blue lines with triangles. Warm fronts are indicated by red lines with half circles. The fronts are moving in the direction of the triangles or half circles. On the map you can see a cold front moving through Oklahoma and just starting to move through Arkansas. If you lived in Arkansas, you could expect that cooler weather would soon reach you. The map shows a warm front moving through Tennessee up toward Kentucky. If you lived in Kentucky, you could expect warmer weather to arrive soon. The yellow area indicates rain. According to the map, what is the weather like in Chicago?

CONTEXT CLUES
Reread paragraph 11. Circle the details that help you understand the meaning of the word fronts.

CHARTS How does the chart on this page help you understand what the text says about fronts?

Types of Fronts	
warm front	a mass of warm air moving toward an area of cooler air
cold front	a mass of cool air moving toward an area of warmer air

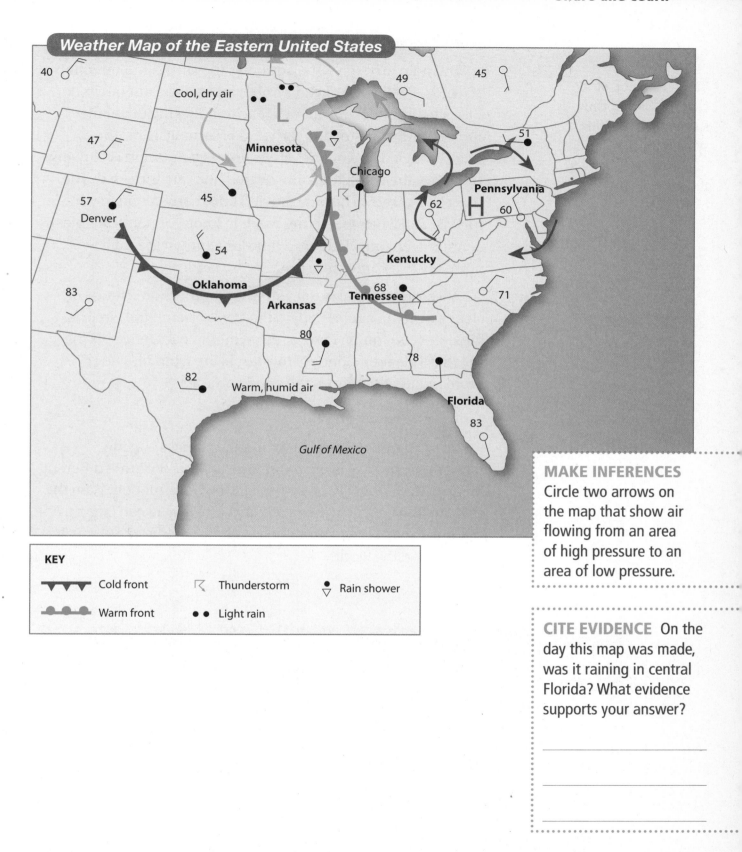

Weather Map of the Eastern United States

40

Cool, dry air

L

47

Minnesota

57
Denver

45

54

Oklahoma

83

Arkansas

82

Warm, humid air

Gulf of Mexico

49

45

51

Chicago

Pennsylvania

62   H   60

Kentucky

68
Tennessee

80

78

Florida

71

83

KEY

▼▼▼ Cold front   ⌐ Thunderstorm   • Rain shower

⬤⬤⬤ Warm front   •• Light rain   ▽ Rain shower

MAKE INFERENCES
Circle two arrows on the map that show air flowing from an area of high pressure to an area of low pressure.

CITE EVIDENCE On the day this map was made, was it raining in central Florida? What evidence supports your answer?

_____

_____

_____

The map on page 131 also shows the speed and direction of winds. Each wind speed symbol looks like a dot or circle with a feather sticking out of it. The line sticking out of the circle shows the direction the wind is coming from. The smaller angled line or lines show how fast the wind is blowing. The faster the wind, the more angled lines are included. The chart below shows how the angled lines correspond to wind speeds. The wind speeds are given in knots, or nautical miles per hour. A nautical mile is a little longer than the mile we normally use to measure distance on land.

These symbols also tell you whether there are clouds or clear sky. If the circle is open, the sky is clear. If the circle is filled in, it is cloudy. Look at the symbol near Denver. Is the sky there clear or cloudy? How fast is the wind blowing? From which direction is the wind coming?

Finding Weather Maps

You can find weather maps in many places—in the newspaper, on television, or on the Internet. There are different kinds of maps that give different kinds of information. With the information you have learned in this article, you can begin to use these maps to see what the weather is doing where you live and around the world.

CHARTS Look at the chart of wind speed symbols. What is the symbol for calm, or no wind? What is the symbol for winds of 50 knots?

Wind Speed Symbols					
Symbol	**Speed**	**Symbol**	**Speed**	**Symbol**	**Speed**
○	Calm	○⌐	20 knots	○⌐	40 knots
○⌐	5 knots	○⌐	25 knots	○⌐	45 knots
○⌐	10 knots	○⌐	30 knots	○⌐	50 knots
○⌐	15 knots	○⌐	35 knots	○⌐	55 knots

Key
5 knots
10 knots
50 knots

Anchor Standard Discussion Questions

Discuss the following questions with your peer group. Then record your answers in the space provided.

1. Describe the structure of the article "Reading a Weather Map." Why do you think the author chose to organize the article in this way? Support your answer with details from the text.

_____

_____

_____

_____

_____

_____

2. Look back at the weather map on page 127, and find the state in which you live. Does the map contain enough information for you to know whether it rained in your state that day? Support your answer with details from the article.

_____

_____

_____

_____

_____

_____

Comprehension Check

1. How do meteorologists gather the information that is used to create a weather map? Use information from both selections you have read in your answer.

2. How is the ability to identify high- and low-pressure areas important to understanding the conditions shown on a weather map?

3. Would it be better to go to the beach on a day of high pressure or low pressure? Explain why.

Read On Your Own

Read another technical text, "Tropical Storms," independently. Apply what you learned in this lesson and check your understanding.

Writing Personal Narratives

If you like an activity, you'll probably do it often enough to get better at it. But what happens if an activity you like is difficult? Would you give it up? Or would you try harder to improve at it? Think about an activity that you especially like. It might be a sport, a craft, or a game. Why do you like it? Do you want to get better at doing it? Have you ever been discouraged by it or felt like giving it up? What made you keep going? How could you share your experience with others? One way would be to write a personal narrative.

ESSENTIAL QUESTION

How can a personal narrative be entertaining and helpful?

What's a Personal Narrative?

Perhaps you enjoy snorkeling, even though you were once stung by a jellyfish. Maybe you play a sport successfully, even though you are not as strong or as fast as some of your peers. Or perhaps you play music, even though you are nervous about playing in front of other people. All of these experiences could be written about as personal narratives.

In a **personal narrative**, you tell about an event or series of events that happened to you. You share what you learned from that experience with others. The flow chart below describes some ways to make your personal narrative effective.

Beginning
Introduce the event, the people involved, and the setting.
Include details that will make readers want to read more.

Middle
Describe events as they happened, from beginning to end. Build suspense and interest with engaging dialogue and vivid description.

Ending
Complete the narrative by summarizing what you learned from the experience.

Let's look at a personal narrative.

Analyze a Mentor Text

This is an example of an effective personal narrative by a fifth grader. Read it and then complete the activities in the boxes with your classmates.

A Word at a Time

When I was younger, I wanted to read chapter books like my older sister did. Her books were really hard to read, but she could read them straight through. She could even recite some of them, retelling whole pages from memory.

After I listened to her read, I thought I would never finish reading anything but a storybook. When I tried to read her books, I always had to ask, "How do you say this word?" or, "What does that word mean?" There were lots of unadorned pages, unlike those in my storybooks that were decorated with illustrations and designs.

But then my mom told me that chapter books were for older kids like my sister, and that was why the words were complex and the books were longer. She said, "You're really good at reading your storybooks."

After that, she said, "You knew some of the words in your storybooks before you read them for the first time, but you had to learn some new ones, too, right?" What really surprised me was when she said, "If I'm reading a challenging book, I sometimes need a dictionary."

I felt better. My parents said the majority of the books at home might be too easy or too hard for me. I asked if we could go to the bookstore and get books that would be just right for me. That Saturday, my dad and I went to the public library and borrowed some chapter books for me to practice reading with.

BEGINNING The opening paragraphs introduce the author's experience and the characters who will be part of the narrative. Circle the sentence that tells the experience the author will write about.

SEQUENCE OF EVENTS The writer narrates events in time order, or chronological sequence. Underline the phrases that show the passage of time.

After a few months, my dad said that I was reading my books very skillfully. Then he brought out my sister's chapter books again. He said, "Shawn, I think you will excel at reading these, don't you?" At first, it was a slow process, but I kept working at it. Eventually, I read all of them! I was really proud when I finished the last one. I said to myself, "Yes, I can!"

When I read them, I didn't know every word, but I didn't feel bad about it. I just asked for help if there was something I struggled with. Reading a challenging book means I get to learn new words and how to pronounce them. If a book is hard to understand, it doesn't mean I'm not a capable reader.

I had been afraid that I didn't have enough vocabulary to be good at reading. But what I have learned is that the more reading I do, the more vocabulary I develop, and the better reader I become!

Think About It ▶ What purpose do you think the author had in mind when describing this experience?

Do you think the reader is likely to want to put more effort into accomplishing a difficult activity after reading this narrative? Why or why not?

Vocabulary Study: Context Clues

The writer says his sister could *recite* her books. If you don't know the meaning of *recite*, you can look for context clues, which are words nearby that help you figure out the unknown word. One context clue is the word *retelling*. *Retell* is a **synonym** of *recite*, or a word that has a similar meaning. An **antonym** is a word that has the opposite meaning of another word. If you don't know the meaning of *unadorned*, the antonym *decorated* can help you figure it out. Thinking about synonyms and antonyms, and watching for them when you read, can often help you figure out words that are unfamiliar.

In the following sentences, circle the word that is a synonym or antonym of the underlined word or phrase.

1. If you have a <u>cheerful</u> attitude, you will find that others around you are usually happy.

2. If you are contrary, it tends to make other people <u>uncooperative</u>.

3. It is hard to trust someone you <u>suspect</u> of acting dishonestly.

4. <u>Focus on</u> the good things in life, and try to overlook the problems.

Complete each sentence using a word or phrase that is a **synonym** of the underlined word.

5. The teacher wants us to <u>recite</u> something in class. I am going to _____ a poem about a river.

6. Learning to fly an airplane is a <u>challenging</u> process. There are many _____ skills that a beginning pilot must master.

7. The story was a comedy about an <u>awkward</u> detective who is so _____ that he trips over his own feet.

Complete each sentence using a word or phrase that is an **antonym** of the underlined word.

8. The math problems in my brother's book are simple. I'm used to more _____ math problems.

9. Can you <u>lend</u> your book to me when you're done reading it? I would like to _____ it for my vacation.

10. The acrobat was _____ of amazing feats, but she was <u>unable</u> to teach others how to do them.

Writing Process

Now that you have read and analyzed a personal narrative, you are going to create your own by following these steps of the writing process.

1. Get Ready: Brainstorm List several challenging activities you might want to write about. Choose an experience to write about in your narrative.

2. Organize Use a graphic organizer to organize events and details and to plan your narrative.

3. Draft Create the first draft of your personal narrative.

4. Peer Review Work with a partner to evaluate and improve your draft.

5. Revise Use suggestions from your peer review to revise your personal narrative.

6. Edit Check your work carefully for spelling, punctuation, and grammar errors.

7. Publish Create a final version of your personal narrative.

Writing Assignment

In this lesson, you will write your own personal narrative. As you create this narrative, remember the elements of the mentor text that were most effective. Read the following assignment.

Write about a skill or trick that you learned, and tell how you learned it. Describe the problems you encountered when learning it, and tell how you finally were successful.

1. Get Ready: Brainstorm a Topic

The first step in writing a personal narrative is to choose your topic. Begin by listing several activities that have challenged you and from which you have learned something. For each one, write what you would like to share about it.

Here's how the author of the mentor text brainstormed topics.

chess	reading	snowboarding
I felt confused when I was learning to play chess, but now it's one of my favorite games.	I wasn't always a confident reader, but I look for challenges now.	I like snowboarding even though I broke my wrist doing it last year.

Try It! Use a Graphic Organizer

Now use the chart below to help brainstorm topics for your own personal narrative. Choose the skill or trick that you enjoy most.

Brainstorm Ideas for Your Topic

You can use a graphic organizer to help brainstorm ideas and details for your personal narrative. Here is how the author of the mentor text used the graphic organizer.

BEGINNING Start by explaining the activity. Get the reader's attention.

MIDDLE Think about which events to include. You can put these events in the best order later. For now, just write down the important things that you remember.

DETAILS Add details to help your reader see and experience what happened. What bits of conversation could you add? What humor could you include?

ENDING Summarize what you learned from your experience.

Beginning	Details
I wanted to read chapter books like my older sister did. I thought I would never finish reading anything but a storybook.	My sister could easily read and even recite from her books. I had to ask how to pronounce words correctly. I had to ask about word meanings.
Middle: Event My mom told me that chapter books were for older kids like my sister.	My sister's books were longer and had more challenging vocabulary than my books.
Middle: Event My parents said the majority of the books at home might be too easy or too hard for me.	I asked if we could go to the bookstore. We went to the library instead.
Middle: Event My dad told me I was doing a good job reading more difficult books.	I didn't know every word, but I didn't feel bad. I asked for help if I didn't understand something.
Ending I used to be afraid that I didn't have enough vocabulary to be good at reading.	If a book is hard to understand, it doesn't mean I'm not a capable reader. The more reading I do, the more vocabulary I develop.

Try It!

Use a Graphic Organizer for Brainstorming

Now use the events chart below to brainstorm your beginning, middle, and ending for your own personal narrative.

Beginning	Details
Middle: Event	
Middle: Event	
Middle: Event	
Ending	

2. Organize

You are almost ready to begin a draft of your personal narrative. You can use a graphic organizer to help organize the events and details you gathered during brainstorming. You can then refer to the graphic organizer as you work through the different parts of your draft. The writer of the mentor text completed this graphic organizer.

BEGINNING In the opening paragraphs, you

- tell the topic of your personal narrative
- include details that make readers want to read more

MIDDLE In the middle paragraphs, you

- tell events in the order in which they happened
- show what the activity is like and how you feel about it, using dialogue and details that will interest your reader

ENDING Your ending should

- summarize what you've learned
- show how you feel about the experience

Beginning
I wanted to read chapter books like my sister, but I had to ask a lot of questions, and it was discouraging.

Middle: Event 1
My mom said that chapter books were for older kids like my sister. They were longer and more difficult. She told me that even she uses a dictionary sometimes.

Middle: Event 2
My parents said the majority of the books at home might be too easy or too hard for me. I asked if we could go to the bookstore. We went to the library.

Middle: Event 3
My dad said I was doing a good job reading more difficult books. I didn't know every word, but I didn't feel bad. I asked for help if I needed it.

Ending
I used to be afraid that I didn't have enough vocabulary to be good at reading—but the more reading I do, the more vocabulary I develop!

Try It!

Organize Your Personal Narrative

Now use the graphic organizer below to organize the ideas and details you want to include in the different paragraphs of your draft.

Beginning

Middle: Event 1

Middle: Event 2

Middle: Event 3

Ending

3. Draft

Now it is time to begin the first draft of your personal narrative. Remember, your draft does not have to be perfect! This is the time to use your notes, write your experience down in an organized way, and have fun. You will have time to revise your writing later. Start by drafting your narrative on a computer or on a separate sheet of paper.

Writer's Craft: Using Transitional Words and Phrases

Transitional words and phrases help writing flow smoothly. They also help readers understand how events are connected. Here are some common transitional words and phrases that help to link events in a time sequence.

Transitional words	**first, next, then, while, later, during, last, meanwhile, afterward, consequently, finally**
Transitional phrases	**on the first day, in the beginning, after a while, the next step, a few days later, last week, later on, one afternoon (or morning, evening), once in a while, at the same time, as a result, at the end**

The author of the mentor text uses transitional words and phrases to begin the first, second, third, fourth, and sixth paragraphs.

TRANSITIONAL PHRASES Read this section of the mentor text. Circle the transitional phrase that introduces the event. Underline the other transitional words or phrases in the paragraph.

> After a few months, my dad said that I was reading my books very skillfully. Then he brought out my sister's chapter books again. He said, "Shawn, I think you will excel at reading these, don't you?" At first, it was a slow process, but I kept working at it. Eventually, I read all of them! I was really proud when I finished the last one.

Try It!   **Write Your First Draft**

On a computer or a separate sheet of paper, continue the draft of your personal narrative. Remember to use transitional words and phrases to show the order of events. Use this drafting checklist to help you as you write.

✓ A good beginning gets your reader's attention. You can begin with a question, a quotation, or an interesting or funny detail.

✓ Be sure to state your topic in the opening paragraph.

✓ Organize events in the order in which they happened.

✓ Use transitional words or phrases to link events.

✓ Include lively details and dialogue to make your writing interesting for the reader.

✓ At the end, summarize what you learned from the experience. Try to write an ending that your readers will remember.

Tips for Writing Your First Draft

- Talk with a classmate about your topic. Explain what you learned from the activity. Encourage the classmate to ask you questions. This is a great warm-up to get you started!

- Write down key phrases and ideas before you begin writing.

- In a personal narrative, your feelings are especially important, so think about why the activity or experience is important to you. Add more details when you revise and edit later.

4. Peer Review

After you finish your draft, you can work with a partner to review each other's drafts. Here is a draft of the mentor text. Read it with your partner. Together, answer the questions in the boxes. Then we'll see how the writer's classmate evaluated the draft.

An Early Draft:

I'll Never Get It!

I wanted to read like my older sister. But her books were really hard. She could read them straight through and out loud with no problem.

I thought I would never finish reading anything but a storybook. I had to ask how do you say this? Or what does that mean? There were so many pages and almost no pictures. I remember trying to read like my sister. I thought I couldn't do it.

My mom told me that chapter books were for older kids and that was why the words were harder and that's why the books were longer. She told me I was really good at reading my storybooks.

She said I knew some of the words in the storybooks before I read the stories for the first time. But I had to learn some new ones, too. She said when she reads a challenging book she needs a dictionary sometimes.

My parents said most of the books at home might be too easy or too hard for me. I asked if we could go to the bookstore. That Saturday, my dad and I went to the public library and got some chapter books for me to practice.

After a while my dad said that I was reading my books very skillfully, and he brought out my sister's chapter books again. He said I'm sure you will excel at reading these too. It took some time but I read them all. I was really proud when I finished the last one.

BEGINNING In this draft, the writer does not give us a sense of when this experience occurred. How did the writer give us a better sense of timing in the finished narrative?

MIDDLE Transitional words and phrases make the order of events clearer. What transitional word or phrase could you add to the third paragraph? What word or phrase could you add to the beginning of the fourth paragraph?

ENDING The conclusion does not summarize what the writer learned from the experience. How would you summarize what the writer learned?

A Sample Peer Review Form

This peer review form gives an example of how a classmate evaluated the draft of the mentor text shown on the last page.

The beginning states the subject in an interesting way.	You did a good job of introducing something you wanted to achieve and sharing your feelings about it.
The writer describes the challenge and tells why it is important.	You could improve your personal narrative by providing more introduction. When does this narrative begin? Did it happen a long time ago or more recently?

The writer describes events in the order in which they happened.	You did a good job of telling what happened when you tried to read your sister's books just like she did.
The writer includes interesting details and dialogue.	You could improve your narrative by giving more details about the books in the second paragraph and adding some dialogue.

The writer uses transitional words and phrases to show when events happened and to make the writing flow smoothly.	You did a good job of putting events in order to tell your story.
	You could improve your narrative by adding transitional words to relate one paragraph to the next and to show how time passed during this experience.

The ending tells what the writer learned from the experience.	You did a good job of sharing your feelings about successfully reading your sister's chapter books.
The ending gives a detail that shows how the writer feels about the experience.	You could improve your narrative by summarizing what you learned from the experience.

Try It!   Peer Review with a Partner

Now you are going to work with a partner to review each other's personal narrative drafts. You will use the peer review form below. If you need help, look back at the mentor text writer's peer review form for suggestions.

The beginning states the subject in an interesting way.	You did a good job of
The writer describes the challenge and tells why it is important.	You could improve your personal narrative by

The writer describes events in the order in which they happened.	You did a good job of
The writer includes interesting details and dialogue.	You could improve your personal narrative by

The writer uses transitional words and phrases to show when events happened and to make the writing flow smoothly.	You did a good job of
	You could improve your personal narrative by

The ending tells what the writer learned from the experience.	You did a good job of
The ending gives a detail that shows how the writer feels about the experience.	You could improve your personal narrative by

Try It! Record Key Peer Review Comments

Now it's time for you and your partner to share your comments with each other. Listen to your partner's feedback, and write down the key comments in the left column. Then write some ideas for improving your draft in the right column.

My review says that my introduction	I will
My review says that my sequence of events	I will
My review says that my use of details	I will
My review says that my use of transitional words	I will
My review says that my ending	I will

Use the space below to write anything else you notice about your draft that you think you can improve.

5. Revise

In this step of the writing process, you work on parts of your draft that need improvement. Use the peer review form that your classmate completed to help you. Also use your own ideas about how to improve each part of your personal narrative. This checklist includes some things to think about as you get ready to revise.

Revision Checklist

✔ Does my beginning catch the reader's interest? Do I describe the challenge?

✔ Are events presented in the order in which they happened?

✔ Do I use details, facts, and dialogue to explain the challenge?

✔ Is my ending interesting? Have I told what I've learned?

✔ Do I use transitional words and phrases to show when the events happened?

✔ Do I use effective punctuation to make my ideas as clear as possible?

Writer's Craft: Using Effective Punctuation

The correct use of commas can clarify your writing. You should use a comma to:

- separate an introductory element from the rest of the sentence ("If you work at it, you will succeed.")
- indicate direct address ("Elena, I know you can do this.")
- set off the words *yes* or *no* ("Yes, I can.")
- set off a tag question ("You did it, didn't you?")

Now look at the mentor text for examples of comma use.

EFFECTIVE PUNCTUATION Circle commas that set off introductory elements. Put a checkmark by commas that indicate direct address, set off a tag question, or set off the word *yes*.

> After a few months, my dad said that I was reading my books very skillfully. Then he brought out my sister's chapter books again. He said, "Shawn, I think you will excel at reading these, don't you?" At first, it was a slow process, but I kept working at it. Eventually, I read all of them! I was really proud when I finished the last one. I said to myself, "Yes, I can!"

Try It!

Revise Your Personal Narrative

Checking for effective punctuation is an important part of revising. The paragraph below contains eight punctuation errors. Can you find them? Write the corrected paragraph in the box below. Then check your own writing carefully for effective punctuation.

> After school I take the bus to my singing class. One day I missed the bus because I was playing with my friends. Luckily there was another bus, but I arrived late. I thought my singing teacher would be angry. To my surprise she just said, "Marco I'm glad you're here. I was worried about you. Please try to be on time. However if you are late, call and tell me will you?" I said, "Yes I will."

Writing Assignment

Now it's time to revise the draft of your personal narrative. Continue working on a computer or on a separate sheet of paper. Review the assignment, repeated below, and the checklist. Doing so will help you make sure that you have included everything you need.

> Write about a skill or trick that you learned, and tell how you learned it. Describe the problems you encountered when learning it, and tell how you finally were successful.

6. Edit

After revising your personal narrative, you will edit it. When you edit, you read very carefully to be sure to find any mistakes in your writing. Here's a checklist of some things to look for as you edit.

> **Editing Checklist**
>
> ✔ Did you indent each paragraph?
>
> ✔ Are all of your sentences complete? Does each have a subject and a verb?
>
> ✔ Did you begin each sentence with a capital letter?
>
> ✔ Does each sentence end with the correct punctuation?
>
> ✔ Have you used commas correctly?
>
> ✔ Are all of your words spelled correctly?

You can use these editing marks to mark any errors you find.

| ⌃ Add | ~~delete~~ Delete | ⊔ Reverse the order |

This paragraph from an early draft of the mentor text shows how to use editing marks.

said
My parents ⌃ most of the books at home might be too easy or too ~~too~~ hard for me. I asked if we could go to the bookstore. That Saturday my dad and I went to the library│public and got some ~~some~~ chapter books for me to practice.

Language Focus: Perfect Tense

The writer of the mentor text says, "What I have learned is . . . ." The verb *have learned* is in the **present perfect tense**. It describes an action that began at an indefinite time in the past. The **past perfect tense** describes an action that happened in the past before some other event. The **future perfect tense** describes an action that will occur in the future before some other event.

Read the examples of the perfect tense in the chart.

Present Perfect Tense	I **have gone** to the library three times this week.
Past Perfect Tense	I **had gone** to the library three times before my favorite book was returned.
Future Perfect Tense	I **will have gone** to the library six times by the end of the month.

1. I feared I couldn't read a whole book, but by that summer, I <u>read</u> five. _____

2. After we go to the library, we <u>have made</u> _____ _____ five trips out of the house today.

3. I have finished reading a new book, so I <u>will have read</u> _____ a total of five books this month.

VERB TENSE Read these statements.

In each statement, the verb tense is incorrect. Write the correct form of the perfect tense on the line after each verb.

Try It! Language and Editing Practice

Underline the correct verb tense for each sentence.

1. If we get to the championships, our team (have / will have) had an almost perfect season.

2. James (has / had / will have) been waiting for fifteen minutes when his father arrived to pick him up.

3. I'm back from the amusement park now, so I (have / had / will have) gone there three times!

Now use editing marks to correct the errors in this paragraph.

Last year was our best baseball season ever. When the season ended, our team winned twelve games. We had only lost eight games. This year we get an even better start. We have won nine of our first ten games. If we keep up this pace, we will win eighteen games when this season ends.

Try It!   **Edit Your Personal Narrative**

Now edit your personal narrative. Use this checklist and the editing marks you have learned to correct any errors you find.

- ☐ Did you indent each paragraph?

- ☐ Are all of your sentences complete? Does each have a subject and a verb?

- ☐ Did you use transitional words to show a clear sequence of events?

- ☐ Does each sentence begin with a capital letter?

- ☐ Have you used effective punctuation? Are commas used correctly?

- ☐ Are all of your words spelled correctly?

Editing Tips

- Read your writing aloud to yourself or to a classmate. This will help you discover missing words and awkward phrases. Ask yourself, "Did that sound right?"

- Listen carefully for stops and pauses as you read. Stops and pauses usually indicate places where punctuation might go. Ask yourself, "Am I missing any commas?"

- Read your writing over at a slow pace at least two times. When reading for small details, one reading is not enough!

7. Publish

On a computer or a separate sheet of paper, create a neat final draft of your personal narrative. Correct all errors that you identified while editing your draft. Be sure to give your personal narrative an interesting title.

The final step is to publish your personal narrative. Here are some different ways you might choose to share your work.

- Read aloud your personal narrative to your class or to a small group of your classmates.

- Gather your personal narrative and the work of your classmates into a booklet.

- Create a bulletin board display with your class's personal narratives.

- Illustrate your narrative with drawings or photographs.

Technology Suggestions

- Upload your personal narrative onto your class or school blog.
- Print out your personal narrative using decorative borders or paper.
- Send your personal narrative as an e-mail to a friend or family member.

Lesson 8

Reading Poetry

Look at this photograph of a lake.

What words would you use to describe the scene? What story could you tell with those words?

ESSENTIAL QUESTION

How can a poem tell a story in a unique way?

What do you like to do outdoors?

Consider ▶ How is catching a fish like a great battle between warriors?

Who will win the battle—the fish or the person fishing?

POETRY A poem is a special kind of writing. In a poem, the author uses the rhythm, sounds, and meanings of words to communicate feelings and ideas in a powerful way. A narrative poem tells a story. Why do you think the author wrote a poem instead of a story about this event?

CONTEXT CLUES Context clues are the words and phrases around an unfamiliar word that can help you figure out its meaning. In stanza 1, the context clues "fishing-line," "to catch," and "King of Fishes" help you figure out that *sturgeon* in line 5 is a kind of fish. What context clues can help you figure out the meaning of the word *craw-fish* in line 14?

Hiawatha's Fishing

from The Song of Hiawatha
by Henry Wadsworth Longfellow

1   Forth upon the Gitche Gumee,
    On the shining Big-Sea-Water,
    With his fishing-line of cedar,
    Of the twisted bark of cedar,
5   Forth to catch the sturgeon Nahma,
    Mishe-Nahma, King of Fishes,
    In his birch canoe exulting
    All alone went Hiawatha.

    Through the clear, transparent water
10 He could see the fishes swimming
    Far down in the depths below him;
    See the yellow perch, the Sahwa,
    Like a sunbeam in the water,
    See the Shawgashee, the craw-fish,
15 Like a spider on the bottom,
    On the white and sandy bottom.

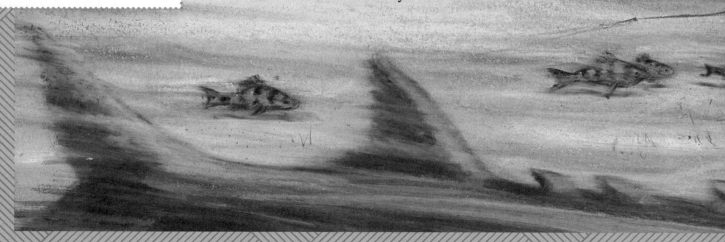

At the stern sat Hiawatha,
With his fishing-line of cedar;
In his plumes the breeze of morning
20 Played as in the hemlock branches;
On the bows, with tail erected,
Sat the squirrel, Adjidaumo;
In his fur the breeze of morning
Played as in the prairie grasses.

25 On the white sand of the bottom
Lay the monster Mishe-Nahma,
Lay the sturgeon, King of Fishes;
Through his gills he breathed the water,
With his fins he fanned and winnowed,
30 With his tail he swept the sand-floor.

STANZA A stanza is to a poem what a paragraph is to a story. A stanza is a series of lines that make up a section of a poem. Like paragraphs, new stanzas indicate shifts in ideas. What is the topic, or idea, of each stanza on this page?

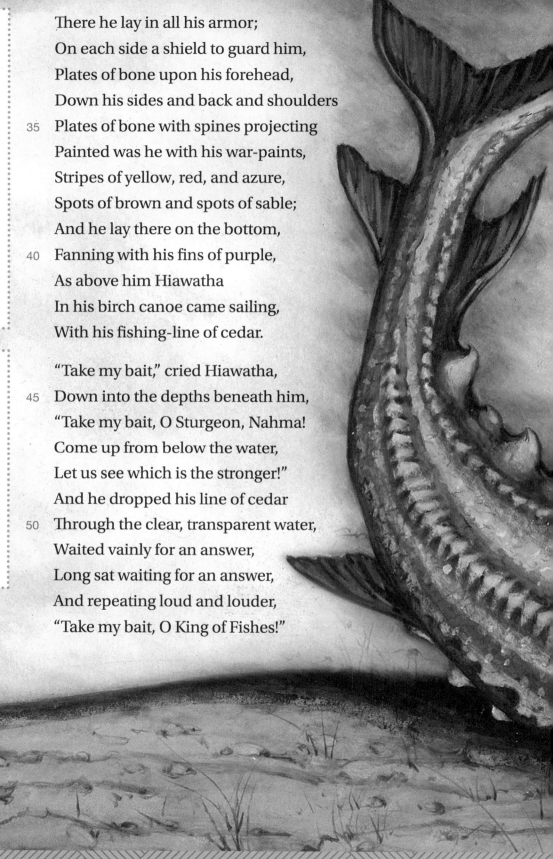

FIGURATIVE LANGUAGE Figurative language is language that uses words to mean something different from their everyday meaning. Poets often use figurative language to describe things in an inventive way. In line 31, the poet says, "There he lay in all his armor." The sturgeon is not really wearing armor. Why do you think the poet describes the fish this way?

METAPHOR A metaphor is a kind of figurative language in which one thing is compared to something different. The sturgeon's stripes are compared to "war-paints." What picture does that form in your mind? What clues to the sturgeon's character does this metaphor give you?

There he lay in all his armor;
On each side a shield to guard him,
Plates of bone upon his forehead,
Down his sides and back and shoulders
35 Plates of bone with spines projecting
Painted was he with his war-paints,
Stripes of yellow, red, and azure,
Spots of brown and spots of sable;
And he lay there on the bottom,
40 Fanning with his fins of purple,
As above him Hiawatha
In his birch canoe came sailing,
With his fishing-line of cedar.

"Take my bait," cried Hiawatha,
45 Down into the depths beneath him,
"Take my bait, O Sturgeon, Nahma!
Come up from below the water,
Let us see which is the stronger!"
And he dropped his line of cedar
50 Through the clear, transparent water,
Waited vainly for an answer,
Long sat waiting for an answer,
And repeating loud and louder,
"Take my bait, O King of Fishes!"

55   Quiet lay the sturgeon, Nahma,

      Fanning slowly in the water,

      Looking up at Hiawatha,

      Listening to his call and clamor,

      His unnecessary tumult,

60   Till he wearied of the shouting;

      And he said to the Kenozha,

      To the pike, the Maskenozha,

      "Take the bait of this rude fellow,

      Break the line of Hiawatha!"

65   In his fingers Hiawatha

      Felt the loose line jerk and tighten,

      As he drew it in, it tugged so

      That the birch canoe stood endwise,

      Like a birch log in the water,

70   With the squirrel, Adjidaumo,

      Perched and frisking on the summit.

SUMMARIZE When you summarize a text, you retell the main ideas in your own words. This is one way to summarize stanza 7: *The sturgeon got bored with listening to Hiawatha and asked another fish to take the bait and break Hiawatha's fishing line.* How would you summarize what happens in stanza 8?

SIMILE A simile is a type of figurative language in which one thing is compared to an unlike thing using the word *like* or *as*. In stanza 8, the birch canoe with one end pointing down under the water and the other end pointing up into the air is "like a birch log in the water." Can you picture the canoe standing on end looking like a birch log? Look back at stanza 2 and find two similes. What two things are being compared in each simile?

LINES Poems and the stanzas in them are made up of lines of words. Lines of poetry often have a similar rhythm, and they may also rhyme. In "Hiawatha's Fishing," each line contains eight syllables. Count the syllables of a few lines. Some stanzas have some lines that rhyme, and others have no rhyming words. Some lines repeat the same word at the end. Which combination of these patterns does the poet use in the lines on this page?

Full of scorn was Hiawatha
When he saw the fish rise upward,
Saw the pike, the Maskenozha,
75 Coming nearer, nearer to him,
And he shouted through the water,
"Esa! esa! shame upon you!
You are but the pike, Kenozha,
You are not the fish I wanted,
80 You are not the King of Fishes!"

Reeling downward to the bottom
Sank the pike in great confusion,
And the mighty sturgeon, Nahma,
Said to Ugudwash, the sun-fish,
85 To the bream, with scales of crimson,
"Take the bait of this great boaster,
Break the line of Hiawatha!"

Slowly upward, wavering, gleaming,

Rose the Ugudwash, the sun-fish,

90 Seized the line of Hiawatha,

Swung with all his weight upon it,

Made a whirlpool in the water,

Whirled the birch canoe in circles,

Round and round in gurgling eddies,

95 Till the circles in the water

Reached the far-off sandy beaches,

Till the water-flags and rushes

Nodded on the distant margins.

But when Hiawatha saw him

100 Slowly rising through the water,

Lifting up his disk refulgent,

Loud he shouted in derision,

"Esa! esa! shame upon you!

You are Ugudwash, the sun-fish,

105 You are not the fish I wanted,

You are not the King of Fishes!"

FIGURATIVE VERSUS LITERAL LANGUAGE

Unlike figurative language, literal language uses words with just their everyday meaning. If the writer had used literal language, he might have said, *Hiawatha dropped his fishing line in the water. The sturgeon ignored the bait, and the sunfish took it instead. Hiawatha reeled in his line. He was angry that he had not caught the sturgeon.* Is this literal story more or less interesting? Why?

Comprehension Check

Think about what happens in the part of the poem "Hiawatha's Fishing" that you just read. (You will be reading more of the poem in the next part of this lesson.) Look back at the stanzas on each page to note the important events. Write the events in the boxes. Then use the events to write a summary of this section of the poem.

Important Ideas and Events, p. 160–161	Important Ideas and Events, p. 162–163	Important Ideas and Events, p. 164–165

SUMMARY

Vocabulary

Use the word map below to help you define and use one of the highlighted vocabulary words from the Share and Learn selection you are about to read or another word you choose.

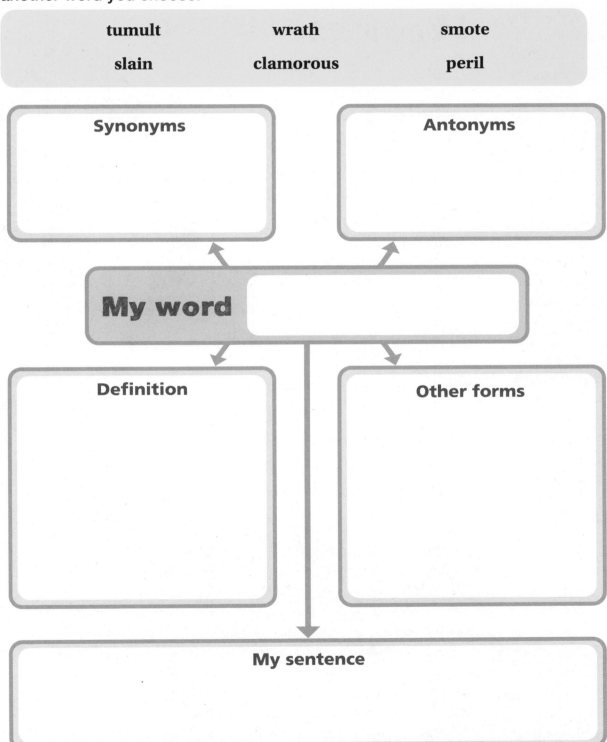

| tumult | wrath | smote |
| slain | clamorous | peril |

Synonyms

Antonyms

My word

Definition

Other forms

My sentence

Consider ▶ Why is Hiawatha determined to catch the sturgeon?

Does facing a challenge make you want to give up or try harder?

STANZA Stanza 2 describes a major turning point, or important change in direction, in the poem. What event marks this turning point?

_____

_____

_____

CHARACTER Nahma the sturgeon is a fierce and powerful character. Circle the words and phrases on this page that build the description of his fierceness and power.

METAPHOR Underline two metaphors in stanza 2. What is being compared? What is the effect of this comparison?

_____

_____

_____

Hiawatha's Fishing

— continued —

1   Slowly downward, wavering, gleaming,
    Sank the Ugudwash, the sun-fish,
    And again the sturgeon, Nahma,
    Heard the shout of Hiawatha,
5   Heard his challenge of defiance,
    The unnecessary tumult,
    Ringing far across the water.

    From the white sand of the bottom
    Up he rose with angry gesture,
10 Quivering in each nerve and fibre,
    Clashing all his plates of armor,
    Gleaming bright with all his war-paint;
    In his wrath he darted upward,
    Flashing leaped into the sunshine,
15 Opened his great jaws, and swallowed
    Both canoe and Hiawatha.

Down into that darksome cavern
Plunged the headlong Hiawatha,
As a log on some black river
20 Shoots and plunges down the rapids,
Found himself in utter darkness,
Groped about in helpless wonder,
Till he felt a great heart beating,
Throbbing in that utter darkness.

25 And he smote it in his anger,
With his fist, the heart of Nahma,
Felt the mighty King of Fishes
Shudder through each nerve and fibre,
Heard the water gurgle round him
30 As he leaped and staggered through it,
Sick at heart, and faint and weary.

SIMILE Find the simile in stanza 3. Draw a box around the two things that are compared.

THEME At first it looks as if Hiawatha has been defeated when he is swallowed by Nahma. But Hiawatha responds to this challenge by striking Nahma's heart with his fist. What does this suggest is the theme of the poem?

_____

_____

_____

CONTEXT CLUES
Reread lines 39 and 40. What context clues help you figure out the meaning of the word *toiled*? Circle them.

LINES How many lines are in each of the stanzas on this page?

_____

In each stanza, underline any words at the ends of lines that are repeated or that rhyme.

Crosswise then did Hiawatha
Drag his birch-canoe for safety,
Lest from out the jaws of Nahma,
35 In the turmoil and confusion,
Forth he might be hurled and perish.
And the squirrel, Adjidaumo,
Frisked and chatted very gayly,
Toiled and tugged with Hiawatha
40 Till the labor was completed.

Then said Hiawatha to him,
"O my little friend, the squirrel,
Bravely have you toiled to help me;
Take the thanks of Hiawatha,
45 And the name which now he gives you;
For hereafter and forever
Boys shall call you Adjidaumo,
Tail-in-air the boys shall call you!"

And again the sturgeon, Nahma,
50 Gasped and quivered in the water,
Then was still, and drifted landward
Till he grated on the pebbles,
Till the listening Hiawatha
Heard him grate upon the margin,
55 Felt him strand upon the pebbles,
Knew that Nahma, King of Fishes,
Lay there dead upon the margin.

Then he heard a clang and flapping,
As of many wings assembling,
60 Heard a screaming and confusion,
As of birds of prey contending,
Saw a gleam of light above him,
Shining through the ribs of Nahma,
Saw the glittering eyes of sea-gulls,
65 Of Kayoshk, the sea-gulls, peering,
Gazing at him through the opening,
Heard them saying to each other,
"'Tis our brother, Hiawatha!"

PLOT At the end of stanza 7 after the battle is finished, the scene has become very calm. What happens in stanza 8 that moves the story along?

_____

_____

_____

FIGURATIVE VERSUS LITERAL LANGUAGE

In stanza 9, the poet uses figurative language to describe the inside of Nahma. Circle the two words he uses. What words would be used in a literal description of the same thing?

_____

_____

CHARACTER Hiawatha says he will reward the seagulls if they help him by giving them a new name, Kayoshk. He says people will forever speak of the gulls' achievements. What does this suggest about Hiawatha's character?

_____

_____

_____

CITE EVIDENCE How does Hiawatha escape from the sturgeon?

_____

_____

Underline the lines that describe his escape.

And he shouted from below them,
70 Cried exulting from the caverns:
"O ye sea-gulls! O my brothers!
I have slain the sturgeon, Nahma;
Make the rifts a little larger,
With your claws the openings widen,
75 Set me free from this dark prison,
And henceforward and forever
Men shall speak of your achievements,
Calling you Kayoshk, the sea-gulls,
Yes, Kayoshk, the Noble Scratchers!"

80 And the wild and clamorous sea-gulls
Toiled with beak and claws together,
Made the rifts and openings wider
In the mighty ribs of Nahma,
And from peril and from prison,
85 From the body of the sturgeon,
From the peril of the water,
They released my Hiawatha.

He was standing near his wigwam,
On the margin of the water,
90 And he called to old Nokomis,
Called and beckoned to Nokomis,
Pointed to the sturgeon, Nahma,
Lying lifeless on the pebbles,
With the sea-gulls feeding on him.

95 "I have slain the Mishe-Nahma,
Slain the King of Fishes!" said he;
"Look! the sea-gulls feed upon him,
Yes, my friends Kayoshk, the sea-gulls;
Drive them not away, Nokomis,
100 They have saved me from great peril
In the body of the sturgeon,
Wait until their meal is ended,
Till their craws are full with feasting,
Till they homeward fly, at sunset,
105 To their nests among the marshes;
Then bring all your pots and kettles,
And make oil for us in Winter."

PARAPHRASE What does Hiawatha say to Nokomis? Write it in your own words.

_____

_____

_____

SETTING In the three stanzas on this page, the setting changes back and forth. What are the two settings portrayed here?

_____

_____

_____

MAKE INFERENCES Why do you think the seagulls stop coming back?

_____

_____

Underline the evidence for your opinion.

SUMMARIZE Write a short summary of the main events that occur after Hiawatha kills Nahma.

_____

_____

_____

And she waited till the sun set,

Till the pallid moon, the Night-sun,

110 Rose above the tranquil water,

Till Kayoshk, the sated sea-gulls,

From their banquet rose with clamor,

And across the fiery sunset

Winged their way to far-off islands,

115 To their nests among the rushes.

To his sleep went Hiawatha,

And Nokomis to her labor,

Toiling patient in the moonlight,

Till the sun and moon changed places,

120 Till the sky was red with sunrise,

And Kayoshk, the hungry sea-gulls,

Came back from the reedy islands,

Clamorous for their morning banquet.

Three whole days and nights alternate

125 Old Nokomis and the sea-gulls

Stripped the oily flesh of Nahma,

Till the waves washed through the rib-bones,

Till the sea-gulls came no longer,

And upon the sands lay nothing

130 But the skeleton of Nahma.

Anchor Standard Discussion Questions

Discuss the following questions with your peer group. Then record your answers in the space provided.

1. What is the poet's opinion of Hiawatha? Do you think the poet views Hiawatha as a hero? Support your answer with evidence from the text.

_____

_____

_____

_____

_____

_____

2. What is Nahma's motivation for attacking Hiawatha? Do you think he was justified in his attack? Support your answer with details from the text.

_____

_____

_____

_____

_____

_____

_____

Comprehension Check

1. The squirrel, Adjidaumo, is swallowed by Nahma along with Hiawatha. What characteristics does Adjidaumo show at this time? Cite evidence from the poem to support your opinion.

   _____

   _____

   _____

2. How does the exchange between Hiawatha and the seagulls benefit both of them?

   _____

   _____

   _____

3. What is the theme of "Hiawatha's Fishing"? How does the poet convey the theme?

   _____

   _____

   _____

Read On Your Own

Read another poem independently. Apply what you learned in this lesson and check your understanding.

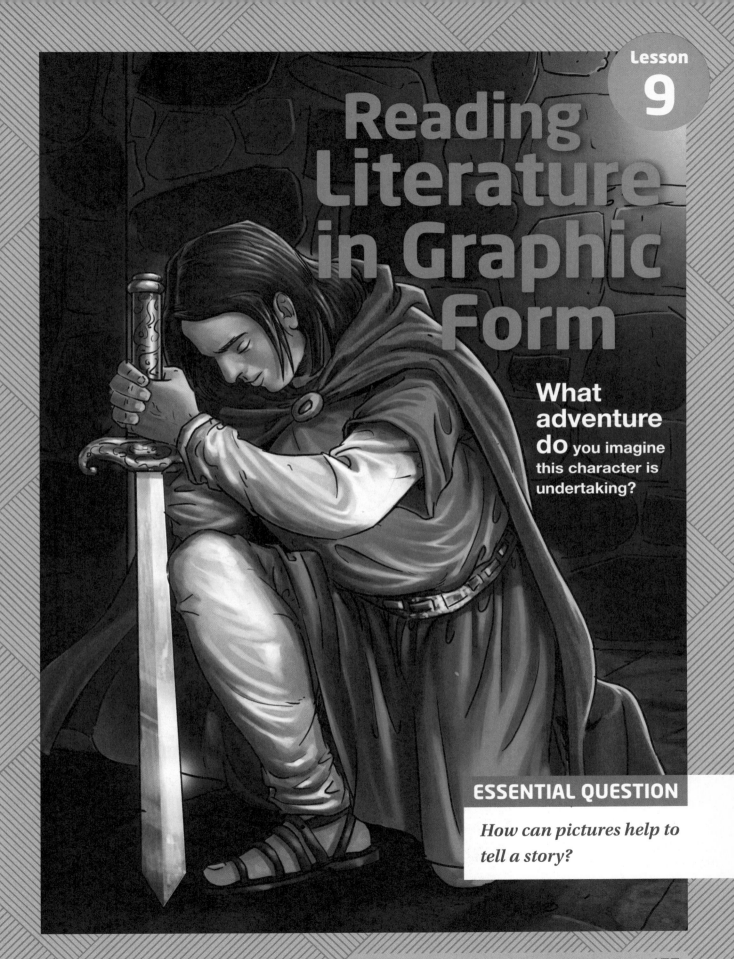

Reading Literature in Graphic Form

What adventure do you imagine this character is undertaking?

ESSENTIAL QUESTION

How can pictures help to tell a story?

Consider ▶ What is honor?

What does an honorable person do in a moment of danger?

Sir Gawain and the Green Knight

GRAPHIC NOVEL Graphic novels use both illustrations and text to tell a story. Illustrations are in boxes called panels. Text is usually in speech balloons (round shapes with a pointer, called a leader, showing who is speaking) or in captions. Readers must combine information from both text and illustrations to follow the story. In the first panel of this graphic story, a great feast is underway. The occasion of the feast is not clear from the illustration. How can you tell the occasion for this celebration?

MAKE INFERENCES
In the second panel of this story, a giant green knight enters the castle hall. The illustration reveals how the others in the hall react. Do you think the knight is an invited guest? How can you infer whether he is invited or not without reading further?

Part 1

Look at the many gifts here this New Year! There is but one thing absent. Let me hear a tale of knightly courage or a distant adventure! Who will answer?

Who is your ruler and hero? Let me have speech with him.

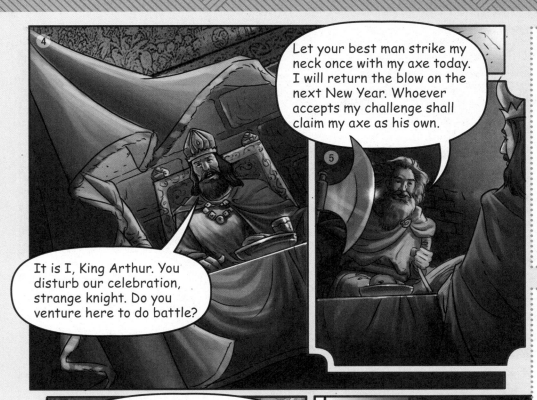

Let your best man strike my neck once with my axe today. I will return the blow on the next New Year. Whoever accepts my challenge shall claim my axe as his own.

It is I, King Arthur. You disturb our celebration, strange knight. Do you venture here to do battle?

MAKE INFERENCES
In panel 7, Sir Gawain takes the knight's challenge, after his king has shown interest in it. Look at where Sir Gawain stands as he accepts the challenge. What does this suggest about the character of Sir Gawain? Why do you think he accepts the challenge?

MAKE INFERENCES
Look at the queen's expression in panel 8. What inference can you make about her feelings at that moment, based on her expression?

Your challenge is as strange as your appearance, Sir knight. I am not young, but I think I shall play at this game of yours.

My lord, permit me! Great knight, I am Sir Gawain of the Round Table, loyal to King Arthur! I accept your challenge. Let us agree to terms.

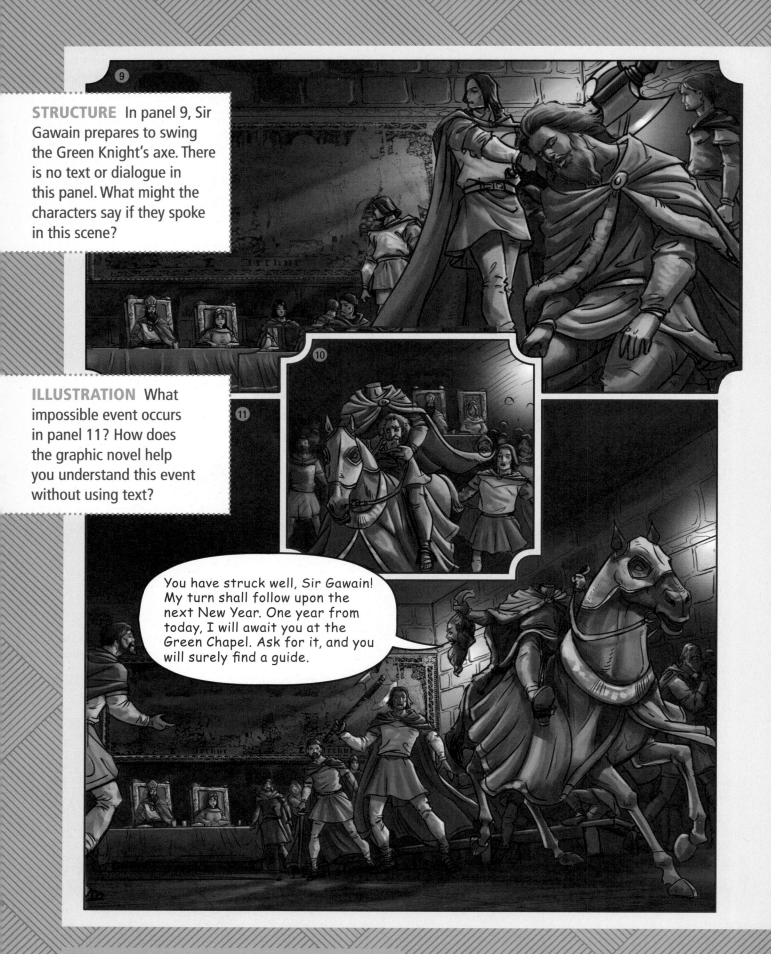

STRUCTURE In panel 9, Sir Gawain prepares to swing the Green Knight's axe. There is no text or dialogue in this panel. What might the characters say if they spoke in this scene?

ILLUSTRATION What impossible event occurs in panel 11? How does the graphic novel help you understand this event without using text?

You have struck well, Sir Gawain! My turn shall follow upon the next New Year. One year from today, I will await you at the Green Chapel. Ask for it, and you will surely find a guide.

MAKE CONNECTIONS
In panel 14, Sir Gawain hangs up the axe he has won by accepting the Green Knight's challenge. How does this action reinforce what Queen Guinevere says in panel 13?

PLOT Based on the plot of the graphic novel so far, what challenge will Sir Gawain face a year from now? What can you infer about Sir Gawain's feelings during the feast?

You make sport of danger, King Arthur.

Guinevere, my queen, it is a season for feats and marvels. Young Sir Gawain has all of a year before he meets this knight. Let us not worry today.

Comprehension Check

One theme of "Sir Gawain and the Green Knight" is that a good person must possess honor and loyalty. In the left column, there are four statements that support this theme. In the right column, cite evidence from pictures or text that support or explain each statement.

Statements that support the theme	Evidence for each statement
Sir Gawain accepts the challenge to protect his king.	King Arthur says he is not young, and Sir Gawain steps in to take the challenge.
The queen fears for Sir Gawain's safety.	
King Arthur and his knights are proud of Sir Gawain for accepting the challenge.	
Sir Gawain plans to keep his bargain with the Green Knight.	

Vocabulary

Use the word map below to help you define and use one of the highlighted vocabulary words from the Share and Learn selection you are about to read or another word you choose.

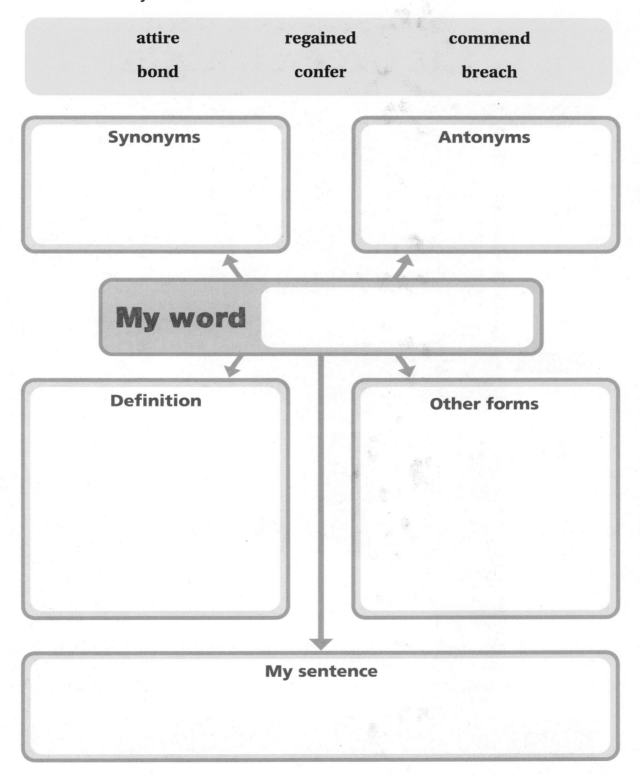

attire   regained   commend

bond   confer   breach

Synonyms

Antonyms

My word

Definition

Other forms

My sentence

Consider ▶ What is temptation?

What does an honorable person do when faced with temptation?

Sir Gawain and the Green Knight

Part 2

SUMMARIZE Before you begin Part 2 of "Sir Gawain and the Green Knight," summarize the major events of Part 1.

MAKE INFERENCES As Part 2 of "Sir Gawain and the Green Knight" begins, Sir Gawain is on a long journey. Where do you think he is going? How much time do you think has passed since the ending of the first part of the story? What in the story makes you think so?

> I am Sir Gawain, knight of the Round Table, and loyal servant to King Arthur of Camelot. I have traveled long and far, eaten little . . . I beg of you shelter, some water . . . perhaps a modest meal is not too much to ask.

> You have come far indeed. I am Lord Bertilak. And this is Lady Bertilak. You are welcome here, Sir Gawain. Let us get you to the fireside and fetch you dry attire. Then, we will dine. When you have regained your strength, tell us of your journey and whatever of its purpose you may share.

THEME In the first part of the story, Sir Gawain made a bargain with the Green Knight that turned out to be more dangerous than he expected. What bargain does Sir Gawain make in this part of the story? How do the two bargains relate to the theme of the story?

_____

_____

_____

PARAPHRASE

Sir Gawain says that King Arthur "is a lover of all manner of sport and jest." In your own words, write what this statement means.

_____

_____

_____

CITE EVIDENCE

In panel 21, where do you think Lord Bertilak is going? What evidence can you cite from the story to support your idea?

_____

_____

_____

PARAPHRASE

Paraphrase what Lady Bertilak says to Sir Gawain in panel 22.

_____

_____

_____

Sir Gawain, may I ask your help? The well head has gone to pieces and must be repaired so the servants may draw their water.

Sir Gawain, please accept this wooden deer for your troubles.

Sir Gawain, I have felled a deer. It is yours, as I promised. Tomorrow I shall hunt again. Shall we keep our agreement another day?

If it pleases you, Lord Bertilak. I thank you—and this is yours.

Good morning, Sir Gawain. Could I trouble you to saddle the mare in the stable today and take her for a run? It keeps her in good health.

Good morning to you, Lady Bertilak. It is no bother to earn my keep while I delay here.

MAKE INFERENCES
Each day, Lady Bertilak asks Sir Gawain to perform a service and then rewards him with a gift. How do you think Sir Gawain feels about Lady Bertilak's gifts? How did you make that inference?

_____

_____

_____

I do not deserve such gifts from the good Lady Bertilak.

You seem deserving. Worry not, Sir Gawain.

Today I have caught a wild boar. What good fortune! It is yours. Let us keep our bond, and I will hunt another day.

And I am to give you this stone figure of a boar.

GRAPHIC NOVEL
Look at panel 30. There are no characters, so there is no dialogue. What information does this panel provide about the story?

_____

_____

_____

THEME In panel 33, Lady Bertilak gives Sir Gawain a silk sash after she offers him a golden statue of a fox and he refuses it. Why do you think he refuses the statue but accepts the sash? How does this add to the development of the theme about loyalty?

_____

_____

_____

MAKE INFERENCES Notice what Lord Bertilak says after Sir Gawain gives him the pin. What can you infer from this about Lord Bertilak's thoughts?

_____

_____

_____

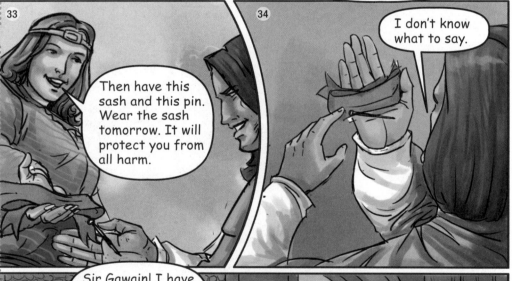

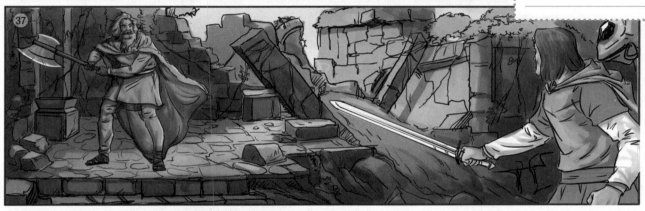

MAKE INFERENCES
What has happened in the story between panels 38 and 39?

_____

_____

_____

SUMMARIZE
Summarize the major events of Part 2 of the story.

_____

_____

_____

THEME What do you think is the message or truth about life that this story suggests?

_____

_____

_____

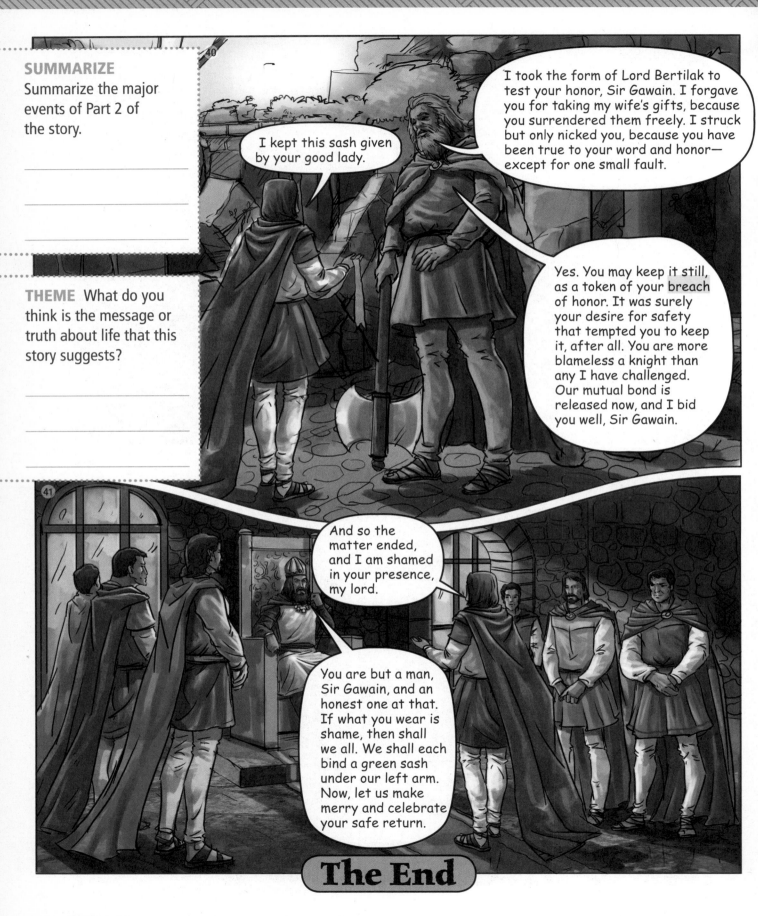

I kept this sash given by your good lady.

I took the form of Lord Bertilak to test your honor, Sir Gawain. I forgave you for taking my wife's gifts, because you surrendered them freely. I struck but only nicked you, because you have been true to your word and honor— except for one small fault.

Yes. You may keep it still, as a token of your breach of honor. It was surely your desire for safety that tempted you to keep it, after all. You are more blameless a knight than any I have challenged. Our mutual bond is released now, and I bid you well, Sir Gawain.

And so the matter ended, and I am shamed in your presence, my lord.

You are but a man, Sir Gawain, and an honest one at that. If what you wear is shame, then shall we all. We shall each bind a green sash under our left arm. Now, let us make merry and celebrate your safe return.

The End

Anchor Standard Discussion Questions

Discuss the following questions with your peer group. Then record your answers in the space provided.

1. Do any illustrations or lines of dialogue foreshadow the surprise that is revealed in panel 40? Support your answer with specific details from the panels in either part of the graphic novel.

_____

_____

_____

_____

_____

_____

2. Create two panels that help readers better understand Sir Gawain's character. Your new scene should take place sometime in the year leading up to Sir Gawain's journey in Part 2. Create your own dialogue and illustrations, and be prepared to support them with details from the graphic novel.

Comprehension Check

1. How is the bargain in Part 2 of the story like the bargain in Part 1? How is it different?

_____

_____

_____

2. How is Sir Gawain's honor tested by Lord and Lady Bertilak, and how does Sir Gawain respond?

_____

_____

_____

3. At the end of the story, King Arthur tells Sir Gawain, "You are but a man, and an honest one at that." Why is this statement important in the story?

_____

_____

_____

Read On Your Own

Read another graphic story independently. Apply what you learned in this lesson and check your understanding.

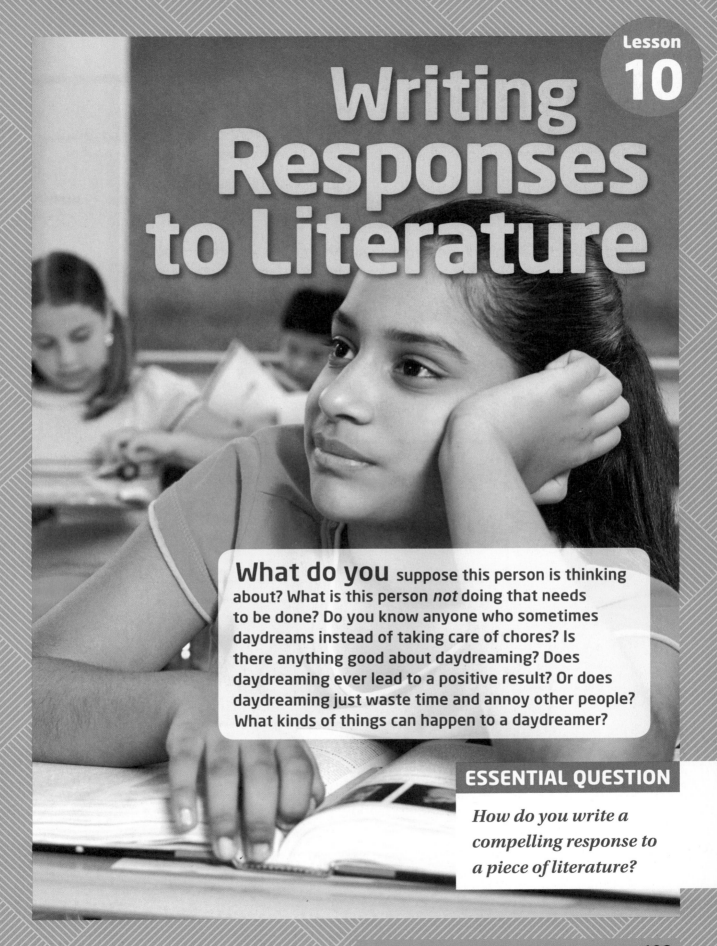

Writing Responses to Literature

What do you suppose this person is thinking about? What is this person *not* doing that needs to be done? Do you know anyone who sometimes daydreams instead of taking care of chores? Is there anything good about daydreaming? Does daydreaming ever lead to a positive result? Or does daydreaming just waste time and annoy other people? What kinds of things can happen to a daydreamer?

ESSENTIAL QUESTION

How do you write a compelling response to a piece of literature?

What's a Response to Literature?

When you read a story, two things you might think about are its setting and characters. Understanding these things helps you understand the story and its message.

To understand the setting of a story, you identify when and where the story takes place. You also think about how the setting affects the action of the story and how the characters act.

To understand the main characters in a story, you pay attention to what the characters say and do. You also notice what the author says about the characters. All of these details give information about the characters.

In a **response to literature**, you describe and analyze one or more aspects of the story, such as its setting and characters. A response to literature is not a summary. Instead, you are writing about specific features of the piece of literature and explaining how they interact. Here are some steps to make your response to literature effective if you are writing about setting or a character.

State the Main Idea
In your first paragraph, tell your readers the title of the story you are writing about. Then tell your topic, or main idea, about the setting or about one of the important characters.

Give Ideas and Details
In the middle paragraphs of your response to literature, give two or three ideas about your topic. Support your ideas with details and examples from the story.

Write a Conclusion
In the last paragraph, restate your main idea and show how your supporting details connect to it.

Let's look at a response to literature.

Analyze a Mentor Text: Reading

The author of the mentor text wrote about the setting of a story. Here is the story the author read and wrote about.

excerpted and adapted from
"Rip Van Winkle" by Washington Irving

Whoever has made a voyage up the Hudson River must remember the Catskill Mountains. The colors and shapes of these mountains are perfect signs of the weather. When the air is fair and settled, they are clothed in blue and purple, and print their bold outlines on the clear evening sky. But when a hood of gray clouds settles on them as the sun goes down, they glow and light up like a crown of glory.

At the foot of these fairy mountains lies a very old village. It was founded by Dutch colonists in the early days of New Netherland (later called New York), when the governor of the colony was Peter Stuyvesant (STY-vuh-sunt). Some of the settlers' houses still stood, built of small yellow bricks brought from Holland. In one of those weather-beaten houses lived a good-natured fellow, of the name Rip Van Winkle. He was a descendant of the Van Winkles who accompanied Governor Stuyvesant to force the Swedes to surrender their small colony, New Sweden, to the Dutch in 1655.

However, Rip did not inherit the fighting character of his ancestors. He was a simple, good-natured man and a kind neighbor. He was a great favorite of all the women of the village. The children, too, would shout with joy whenever he approached. He played sports with them, made them toys, taught them to fly kites and shoot marbles, and told them long stories. Even the dogs liked him. Not a single one would bark at him throughout the neighborhood.

Rip had just one shortcoming, and that was his tendency to avoid any hard work. It could not be because he lacked patience, for without a murmur he could sit on a rock all day with his long gun and hunt squirrels or wild pigeons for hours at a time. He would never refuse to assist with a neighbor's work, and he often performed errands and odd jobs for the women of the village. Rip was ready to attend to anybody's business but his own.

But keeping his own farm in order was impossible. Everything about it went wrong. His fences were continually falling to pieces. His cow would either wander away or get among the cabbages. Weeds were sure to grow quicker in his fields than anywhere else. The rain would begin to fall just as he had some outdoor work to do. Rip's farm was in the worst shape of any in the neighborhood.

Rip Van Winkle, however, was one of those happy people who take the world easy. He would have whistled his life away, in perfect contentment, if not for his wife. Dame Van Winkle was continually dinning in his ears about his idleness, his carelessness, and the ruin he was bringing on his family. Morning, noon, and night, her tongue was always going, and she had something to say about everything Rip did. Rip had only one way of replying to all her lectures. He shrugged his shoulders, shook his head, cast up his eyes, but said nothing. This always caused his wife to start in anew on his failures, so he took it upon himself to leave the house.

Rip's sole friend at home was his dog, Wolf, who was scolded just as much as his master by Dame Van Winkle. She regarded them as companions in idleness, and even blamed Wolf as the cause of his master's going astray. Wolf was as courageous an animal as any in the woods, but the moment he entered the house his spirits fell, and his tail curled between his legs. He sneaked about, casting a sidelong glance at Dame Van Winkle. If she so much as picked up a broomstick or ladle, he would fly to the door with a yelp. "Poor Wolf," Rip would say, "thy mistress leads thee a dog's life of it. But never mind, my lad, while I live thou shalt never want a friend to stand by thee!" Wolf would wag his tail and look wistfully in his master's face.

Analyze a Mentor Text: Response to Literature

Here is an effective fifth-grade response to literature written about the story you just read. The author wrote about the historical setting of "Rip Van Winkle." Read the response and then complete the activities in the boxes as a class.

The Importance of Setting in "Rip Van Winkle"

The Catskill Mountains seem like a strange place. I just finished reading "Rip Van Winkle." This retelling of a famous short story takes place in the Catskill Mountains in the early days of the American colonies. The descriptions of the large and small places in the story and of the time when the story takes place are important. Understanding this setting helps me understand the characters in the story.

The narrator begins by describing the Catskill Mountains, where the story takes place. The mountains appear to change in different kinds of weather. In pleasant weather, they look blue and purple, and their outlines appear clearly in the evening. When it is cloudy, the evening sun lights the clouds so that the mountains look like they have a crown of glory. These descriptions make me think that the mountains seem almost to have some kind of strange power.

The narrator says the characters live in a "very old village" at the foot of the "fairy mountains." Specifically, the narrator says the village was founded by the Dutch at a time when New York was called New Netherland. Also, the settlers brought small yellow bricks with them to build their houses. In addition, we learn that some of Rip Van Winkle's ancestors were in a long-ago battle with the colony of New Sweden. This description makes the village seem strange and far away in time. In fact, it seems like a place where something unusual could happen.

MAIN IDEA The author gives the story's title and states the topic. Circle the title of the story. Underline the sentence that gives the main idea of this response to literature.

IDEAS AND DETAILS What is the physical setting mentioned in paragraph 2 of the story? What does the writer of the mentor text suggest is important about this setting?

IDEAS AND DETAILS Next, the author tells about another aspect of the setting. How does the author suggest this new part of the setting adds to the development of the story?

IDEAS AND DETAILS
What important ideas about setting does the author give in paragraph 4? How does the author say these details help to show what kind of person Rip is?

CONCLUSION In the conclusion, the author sums up her response to the setting. She explains how the setting helps her understand the main character and what she thinks may happen as the story develops.

Other details tell more about the village. It's a busy place, with children and dogs and people working. Rip's neighbors and people in the village often ask him to help with their work or run errands for them. But Rip isn't like others in the village. He helps people, but he doesn't like to work. His farm is in the worst shape of any in the neighborhood. The fields are weedy, and the fences are falling down. Rip's wife also pesters him for not doing more work around their house and farm. These details of the setting help show that Rip is different. In fact, Rip only has one friend at home, his dog, Wolf.

All of these details tell me that the place and time of the story are far away and somewhat strange. They also help me understand that Rip is a kind of stranger in the place where he lives. This makes me think that Rip is probably going to have some kind of strange adventure. And maybe Wolf will be part of it.

Washington Irving, the author of "Rip Van Winkle"

Vocabulary Study: Dialect

Dialect is vocabulary and pronunciation that belongs to a particular time, place, or social group. Dialects in English can generally be understood by any English speaker, but they may seem unusual to people who are unfamiliar with them. Here is a sample of dialect from the American South:

My family is <u>fixin' to</u> go on vacation. (getting ready)
That car <u>doesn't amount to a hill of beans</u>. (isn't worth very much)

Here is a sample of dialect from the Appalachian Mountains:

You done made me forget where I was going.
He was a-tellin' the truth.

Here is a sample of British dialect:

I need to take the <u>lift</u> to the fifth floor. (elevator)
We will move to our new <u>flat</u> on Saturday. (apartment)

Reread "Rip Van Winkle." Find an example of dialect, and write it in the chart below. Then rewrite it using your own words.

Dialect	Dialect Rewritten

Writing Process

You have read and analyzed a response to literature. Now you are going to create your own response to literature by following these steps of the writing process.

1. Get Ready: Brainstorm Think about your topic—in this case, the main characters in "Rip Van Winkle." What do you know about these characters? How are they alike and different?

2. Organize Use a graphic organizer to organize and plan your response to literature.

3. Draft Create the first draft of your response.

4. Peer Review Work with a partner to evaluate and improve your draft.

5. Revise Use suggestions from your peer review to revise your response to literature.

6. Edit Check your work carefully for spelling, punctuation, and grammar errors.

7. Publish Create a final draft of your response.

Writing Assignment

In this lesson, you will write your own response to "Rip Van Winkle." The author of the mentor text analyzed the setting of the story. You will write about the main characters in the story. As you create your response to literature, remember the elements of the mentor text that you found most effective. Read the following assignment.

> The main characters in "Rip Van Winkle" are Rip, his wife, and his dog, Wolf. Compare and contrast these three characters, and explain how their similarities and differences are important to the story.

1. Get Ready: Brainstorm

The first step in writing a response to literature is to choose your topic and decide what part of the topic you want to focus on.

The author of the mentor text responded to a writing assignment about the setting of "Rip Van Winkle." Here's how the author brainstormed about what to focus on.

Aspect of Setting	Details
Place: Catskill Mountains	Changing and powerful
Time: Old village, seems far away in time	Very old, Dutch colonists, long-ago battle
Setting and Character: Busy community, but Rip is different	Rip helps others but doesn't like to work on his own farm.

Try It!　Use a Brainstorming Graphic Organizer

Now use the chart below to help brainstorm what about your topic you want to focus on for your own response to literature.

Character	Traits
Rip Van Winkle	
Dame Van Winkle, Rip's wife	
Wolf, Rip's dog	

Brainstorm Ideas About Your Topic

You can use a graphic organizer to help brainstorm ideas and details for your response to literature. Here is how the author of the mentor text used this graphic organizer to generate ideas about the setting of "Rip Van Winkle."

BEGINNING The author describes different aspects of the setting and how the setting affects the main character.

IDEAS AND DETAILS For each aspect of the setting, the author lists details that are important.

Place	Time	How setting affects the main character
In Catskill Mountains Mountains change in appearance with changes in the weather. They seem to have some kind of strange power. Rip's village is at the foot of the "fairy mountains."	Village is very old, was settled by Dutch colonists. Houses are old, built of yellow bricks the settlers brought. Rip's ancestors fought in a long-ago battle. Village seems lost in time.	Rip's village is full of busy people. Sometimes Rip helps on farms or runs errands. Rip's farm is in bad shape. He doesn't like to work. Rip's wife pushes Rip to work harder on their farm. Rip and his dog feel oppressed.

Try It!

Use a Graphic Organizer for Brainstorming

When comparing and contrasting characters, using a Venn diagram is helpful. Brainstorm details about each of the characters. Place details they have in common in the areas where the circles overlap.

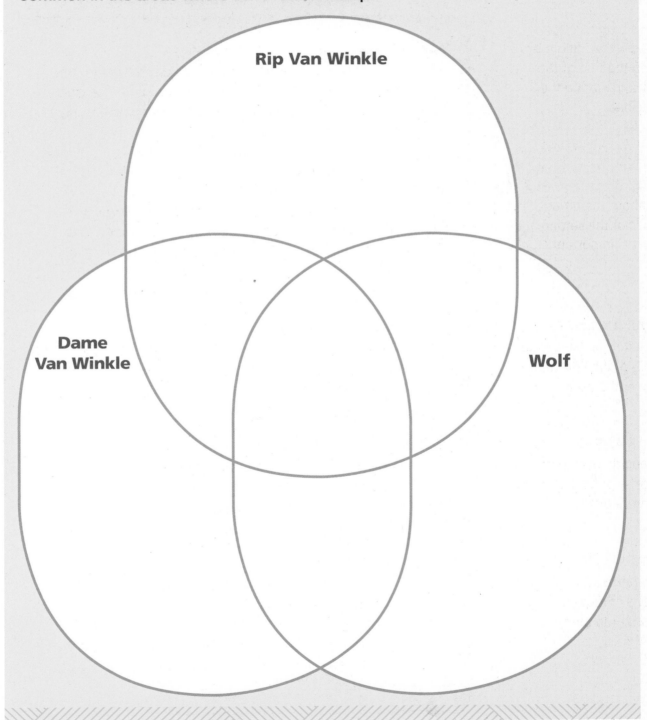

Rip Van Winkle

Dame Van Winkle

Wolf

2. Organize

You are almost ready to begin a draft of your response to literature. You can use a graphic organizer to help you organize your ideas and the details you noted in brainstorming. You can then refer to the graphic organizer as you work through your draft. The writer of the mentor text completed this chart to write her essay.

MAIN IDEA Begin by giving the title of the story and stating the main idea.

IDEAS AND DETAILS Tell about the broad details of the setting and why it is important.

IDEAS AND DETAILS Tell about the more local details of the time and place of the story.

IDEAS AND DETAILS Tell about how the details of the setting relate to the main character.

CONCLUSION Summarize how the three aspects of the setting are important to the story.

Main Idea
The story "Rip Van Winkle" takes place long ago. The setting is a village in the Catskill Mountains in the early days of the American colonies. Understanding the setting helps me understand the characters.

Place
The Catskill Mountains look different depending on the weather. They seem to have a strange power. The village where Rip Van Winkle lives is at the foot of the "fairy mountains."

Time
Rip's village is very old. The houses were built by Dutch colonists. Rip's ancestors fought in a long-ago battle. The village seems lost in time.

Setting and Character
The village is busy with hardworking farmers. But Rip's farm is in bad shape. His wife pesters Rip to work harder. Rip and his dog, Wolf, feel oppressed.

Conclusion
Understanding all aspects of the setting is important. The place and time of the story influence how the main character is depicted. Rip seems to be almost a stranger in his strange village. This makes me think he will have some kind of strange adventure, maybe with his dog, Wolf.

Try It!

Organize Your Response to Literature

Now use the graphic organizer below to plan the draft of your response to literature.

Main Idea

Details About the First Character

Details About the Second Character

Details About the Third Character

Compare and Contrast the Characters

Conclusion

3. Draft

Now it is time to begin the first draft of your response to literature. Remember, your draft does not have to be perfect! This is the time to use your notes, get your ideas down in some sort of organized way, and have fun. You will have time to revise your writing later. Start by drafting your response to literature on a computer or on a separate sheet of paper. Support your statements with details from the story.

Writer's Craft: Using Linking Words and Phrases

Linking words and phrases can help your writing flow smoothly and help readers understand how ideas are connected. Here are some common linking words and phrases:

Linking Words	Linking Phrases
after, also, another, although, because, before, consequently, even, first, finally, however, later, next, other, so, specifically, then, too, when	another cause, at this point, in addition, in fact, in order to, in spite of, without reason, underneath it all

The author of the mentor text uses linking words and phrases in paragraph 3.

LINKING WORDS Read this section of the mentor text. Circle four linking words or phrases.

The narrator says the characters live in a "very old village" at the foot of the "fairy mountains." Specifically, the narrator says the village was founded by the Dutch at a time when New York was called New Netherland. Also, the settlers brought small yellow bricks with them to build their houses. In addition, we learn that some of Rip Van Winkle's ancestors were in a long-ago battle with the colony of New Sweden. This description makes the village seem strange and far away in time. In fact, it seems like a place where something unusual could happen.

Try It!   Write Your First Draft

On a computer or a separate sheet of paper, continue the draft of your response to literature. Remember to use linking words and phrases to connect your ideas. Use this drafting checklist to help you as you write.

✓ A good beginning gets your reader's attention. You can begin with a striking image, a quotation, or an unexpected statement.

✓ Be sure to state the main idea of your response to literature in the first paragraph.

✓ Develop the details about your characters that support the main idea.

✓ Use the ideas and details that you noted in Step 2: Organize.

✓ In your conclusion, explain how the characters' similarities and differences are important to the story.

Tips for Writing Your First Draft

- Try imagining you are talking to friends about the story. This may help you relax and think of new ideas.

- Think about what you would do if you were in your characters' shoes. This may help you understand the characters and how they act.

- If you get stuck, do something routine, like taking out the trash. Sometimes your ideas sort themselves out when you're doing something other than writing.

4. Peer Review

After you finish your draft, you can work with a partner to review each other's drafts. Here is a draft of the mentor text. Read it with your partner. Together, answer the questions in the boxes. Then we'll see how the writer's classmate evaluated the draft.

MAIN IDEA The author mentions three aspects of the setting but does not explain her main idea about the setting. What could she add to make the main idea clearer?

IDEAS AND DETAILS The author does not make clear how the weather makes the Catskill Mountains important to the characters. What details from the story could she add?
The author describes the history and other details of the village but does not tell how these details relate to her main idea. What would you add?

CONCLUSION The author doesn't explain why understanding the setting is important. How could she make her conclusion stronger?

An Early Draft:

The Importance of Setting in "Rip Van Winkle"

I have just finished reading "Rip Van Winkle." The descriptions of the large and small places in the story and of the time when the story takes place are important.

The narrator begins by describing the Catskill Mountains, where the story takes place. The mountains change in different kinds of weather. The mountains are important to the characters in the story.

The characters live in a village at the foot of the mountains. It was founded by the Dutch at a time when the colony of New York was called New Netherland. The settlers brought small yellow bricks with them to build their houses. In addition, we know that some of Rip Van Winkle's ancestors were involved in the military.

Other details tell more about the village. We know that most of the people in the village are farmers. They are also very hard workers. Rip's wife pesters him for not doing more work around their own house and farm.

All of these details about the place and time of the story are important. Knowing about where the story takes place and what its history is helps me read the story.

An Example Peer Review Form

This peer review form gives an example of how a classmate evaluated the draft of the mentor text shown on the previous page.

The beginning identifies the title of the reading selection and the topic.	You did a good job of *identifying the reading selection.*
The writer states the main idea in the first paragraph.	You could improve your response by *stating why the setting is important to the story.*

The writer describes the time and place of the story.	You did a good job of *describing different parts of the setting.*
The writer uses details to show how each aspect of the setting contributes to the story.	You could improve your response by *providing more details to help the reader understand how the setting is important to the story.*

The writer uses linking words and phrases to show how ideas are connected.	You did a good job of *using linking words and phrases like "in addition," "other," and "also."*
Linking words and phrases help the writing flow smoothly.	You could improve your response by *adding linking words like "because" and "specifically" to explain why details about the setting are important.*

The conclusion summarizes why the setting is important to the story.	You did a good job of *telling that the details of place and time are important to the story.*
The writer makes the conclusion interesting for the reader.	You could improve your response by *explaining more clearly how knowing about the setting helps you understand the characters better.*

Try It!

Peer Review with a Partner

Now you are going to work with a partner to review each other's drafts. You will use the peer review form below. If you need help, look back at the mentor text writer's peer review form for suggestions.

The beginning identifies the main characters in "Rip Van Winkle." **The writer states the main idea in the first paragraph.**	You did a good job of You could improve your response by
The writer explains the traits of each character. **The writer shows how the characters are similar to and different from one another.**	You did a good job of You could improve your response by
The writer uses linking words and phrases to show how ideas are connected. **Linking words and phrases help the writing flow smoothly.**	You did a good job of You could improve your response by
The conclusion explains how the characters' similarities and differences are important to the story. **The writer makes the conclusion interesting for the reader.**	You did a good job of You could improve your response by

Try It!

Record Key Peer Review Comments

Now it's time for you and your partner to share your comments with each other. Listen to your partner's feedback, and write down the key comments in the left column. Then write some ideas for improving your draft in the right column.

My review says the beginning	I will
My review says the main idea	I will
My review says the explanation of the characters' traits	I will
My review says the explanation of similarities and differences	I will
My review says that linking words and phrases	I will
My review says the conclusion	I will

Use the space below to write anything else you notice about your draft that you think you can improve.

5. Revise

In this step of the writing process, you work on parts of your draft that need improvement. Use the peer review form that your classmate completed to help you. This checklist includes some things to think about as you get ready to revise.

Revision Checklist

✔ Does my beginning state the topic and the main idea?

✔ Do I describe the details of what the characters say and do?

✔ Do I use linking words and phrases to show how ideas are connected?

✔ Does my writing flow smoothly?

✔ Do I use precise language?

✔ Does my conclusion summarize my ideas about the characters?

Writer's Craft: Using Precise Language

Using precise words makes your writing clearer and more interesting. For example, in the sentence "This character was good at many things," the words *good* and *things* are imprecise. Instead, you might write, "This character was skilled at playing the piano and painting." Now look at the mentor text for examples of precise language.

PRECISE LANGUAGE
Precise language means words that are clear and exact. Underline examples of precise language in this paragraph.

The narrator begins by describing the Catskill Mountains, where the story takes place. The mountains appear to change in different kinds of weather. In pleasant weather, they look blue and purple, and their outlines appear clearly in the evening. When it is cloudy, the evening sun lights the clouds so that the mountains look like they have a crown of glory. These descriptions make me think that the mountains seem almost to have some kind of strange power.

Try It! Revise Your Response to Literature

Checking to be sure you used precise language is an important part of revising. Practice using precise language with the following paragraph. Replace each underlined example of imprecise language with precise language.

> The neighborhood I live in is big. People decorate their houses and lawns with lots of things. Many kinds of vehicles drive through all day long.

Replace *big* with _____

Replace *people* with _____

Replace *things* with _____

Replace *many kinds of vehicles* with _____

_____

Writing Assignment

Now it's time to revise the draft of your response to literature. Continue working on a computer or on a separate sheet of paper. Review the assignment, repeated below, and the checklist. Doing so will help you make sure that you have included everything you need.

> The main characters in "Rip Van Winkle" are Rip, his wife, and his dog, Wolf. Compare and contrast these three characters, and explain how their similarities and differences are important to the story.

6. Edit

After revising your response to literature, you will edit it. When you edit, you read very carefully to find any mistakes in your writing. Here's a checklist of some things to look for as you edit.

> ### Editing Checklist
>
> ✓ Did you indent each paragraph?
>
> ✓ Are all of your sentences complete? Does each have a subject and a verb?
>
> ✓ Did you begin each sentence with a capital letter?
>
> ✓ Does each sentence end with the correct punctuation?
>
> ✓ Have you used commas correctly?
>
> ✓ Are all of your words spelled correctly?

You can use these editing marks to mark any errors you find.

⌃ Add	⊙ Period	≡ Capitalize
∽ Reverse order	~~delete~~ Delete	

This is a paragraph from an early draft of the mentor text showing how to use editing marks.

The narrator begins by ~~by~~ describing the Catskill

mountains, where the story takes place. The mountains

change in different ^Kinds of^ weather. The mountains are important

~~the~~ to characters in the story⊙

Language Focus: Spelling Rules

Reviewing your writing gives you a chance to check your spelling. Here are two spelling rules to review as you edit your response to literature.

1. When forming the plural of a noun that ends in *y*, look to see whether the *y* follows a consonant or a vowel.

Singular Ending	Plural Form	Example
consonant + *y*	Change *y* to *i* and add -*es*.	baby—babies party—parties grocery—groceries
vowel + *y*	Add -*s*.	turkey—turkeys way—ways journey—journeys

2. The |sh| sound may be spelled using the letter combinations *sh*, *ss*, *ci*, or *ti*.

Letter Combination	Example
sh	rush, cushion, share
ss	session, pressure, assure
ci	ancient, appreciate, delicious
ti	fraction, partial, position

I just finished reading "Rip Van Winkle." This retelling of a famous short story takes place in the Catskill Mountains in the early days of the American colonies. The descriptions of the large and small places in the story and of the time when the story takes place are important. Understanding this setting helps me understand the characters in the story.

SPELLING RULES Read these lines from the mentor text. Circle plural words that are formed from a singular word ending in *y*. Draw a box around words that contain the |sh| sound, and notice which combination of letters makes the sound in each word.

Try It! Language and Editing Practice

Complete each sentence using the correct plural form of the word in parentheses.

1. Wilson left his _____ at home today.   (key)

2. I hope we don't have any _____ on our trip.   (emergency)

3. Our team got a lot of _____ during the game.   (penalty)

4. Ashlyn's favorite animals at the zoo are the _____. (monkey)

5. There are many _____ on the lunch menu.   (specialty)

Each of the underlined words in this paragraph is incorrect. Use editing marks to correct the words.

Eliseo brought home a <u>permition</u> slip for his parents to sign. The next day, his

class would go to a school <u>aucshun</u>. The money raised there would be used to

conduct <u>audissions</u> for the next school play. Eliseo was glad. He thought the

play would be <u>benefitial</u> for his school.

Try It!

Edit Your Response to Literature

Now edit your response to literature. Use this checklist and the editing marks you have learned to correct any errors you find.

[ ] Did you indent each paragraph?

[ ] Are all of your sentences complete? Have you corrected fragments and run-ons?

[ ] Did you begin each sentence with a capital letter? Did you capitalize proper nouns and adjectives?

[ ] Does each sentence end with the correct punctuation mark?

[ ] Have you used commas correctly?

[ ] Are all of your words spelled correctly?

[ ] Have you used precise language?

Editing Tips

- Read your writing aloud. This will help you discover missing words and awkward phrases. Ask yourself, "Did that sound right?"

- Try reading your writing backward, one sentence at a time. This may help you catch spelling errors you missed before.

- When you think you are finished editing, read your piece one more time. This can help you catch mistakes you overlooked.

7. Publish

On a computer or a separate sheet of paper, create a neat final draft of your response to literature. Correct all errors that you identified while editing your draft. Be sure to give your response to literature an interesting title.

The final step is to publish your response to literature. Here are some different ways you might choose to share your work.

- Create large portraits of Rip Van Winkle, Dame Van Winkle, and Wolf. Display these portraits on the bulletin board, surrounded with the pieces you and your classmates wrote about the characters.

- Ask if you can display your response to literature on the wall of your classroom or somewhere in the school building.

- Illustrate your response to literature with pictures of characters or events.

- Bind your response to literature with staples or spiral binding, or place it in a folder.

Technology Suggestions

- Upload your response onto your class or school blog.
- Find illustrations of the story of Rip Van Winkle on the Internet and use them to illustrate your work.

Reading Scientific Nonfiction

Look at this picture of northern elephant seals in California. What qualities do you think make these seals different from other seals?

ESSENTIAL QUESTION

How do articles about science and nature differ from narrative stories?

Consider ▶ How do different animals interact with their environment?

How can studying the natural world help improve humans' lives?

Leafcutter Ants

1   Humans have been farming for thousands of years. That seems like a long time, but another animal has been farming much longer. In fact, the oldest farmers on Earth might be insects. Today, we know about a type of ant that has been tending crops for about 50 million years. These ancient farmers are called leafcutter ants.

Leafcutter ants are one of 10,000 types of ants. Each type has qualities that make it different from other types. For example, leafcutter ants are one of the few types of ants that grow their food. They are called leafcutter ants because of the way they use leaves in their farming process. First, they strip leaves off of plants. Then, they carry them back to their colonies. They chew the leaves into a paste. This paste helps the food in their gardens grow.

But the food in these ants' gardens is different from the food in humans' gardens. Humans grow plants in their gardens. Leafcutter ants grow fungus. They live off the fungus they grow and harvest.

Leafcutter ants use leaves from more than eighty kinds of plants to feed their fungus gardens.

Leafcutters and Other Ants

Leafcutter ants are similar to other ants in most ways. Ants, like all insects, have six legs, and their bodies are divided into three sections. They also have a hard outer covering called an exoskeleton instead of bones. Like some other ants, leafcutter ants are dark red and small. The smallest ones are about 2 millimeters wide. The largest can be 20 millimeters wide. Even though they are small, leafcutter ants are very strong. In fact, some can carry six times their own weight. That would be like a human adult carrying a horse.

5   Leafcutters also have features that are different from those of other ants. These features help them do their job as farmers. First, they have three pairs of spikes across their backs. These spikes help the ants carry leaves on their backs like umbrellas. Leafcutters also have two blades that stick out from between their teeth. These blades allow them to cut through leaves easily. On younger ants, the blades are sharper than a razor. However, as the ants grow older, these blades become dull. This makes cutting leaves harder. As a result, older ants have responsibilities other than cutting leaves.

Where Leafcutters Live

Leafcutter ants are found in South America, Central America, Mexico, and the southern United States. Many live in rainforests. Others live in open woodlands and forests. Like many other ants, they live in underground nests. Millions of ants may live in one nest. To hold so many ants, leafcutter ant nests may extend horizontally to 600 square meters and vertically to a depth of 18 meters underground. The group of ants that lives inside one nest is called a colony.

In addition to their great strength, leafcutter ants show tremendous speed as they haul leaf fragments back to their nests.

TRANSITION WORDS
An author will often use words to help the reader understand how two things or ideas are related. To show comparison, a writer will use words such as *similarly* and *also*. To show contrast, words such as *unlike* and *instead* may be used. Words such as *indeed* and *surely* show emphasis. These words are called transition words. In paragraph 4, what words emphasize how strong the ants are? In paragraph 5, what word helps the writer contrast young and old ants?

CAUSE AND EFFECT
Writing that uses cause and effect organizes information by showing why things happen or why things are the way they are. The cause tells what makes something happen, and the effect tells what happens as a result. In paragraph 5, what effect does growing older have on an ant's blades? How does this effect cause something else to happen?

Specialized Types of Leafcutter Ants

PROBLEM AND SOLUTION
Writers of scientific nonfiction often organize their writing by stating a problem and describing its solution. The writer tells us that leafcutter colonies have many needs to meet. What is the solution to this problem?

With millions of ants living in them, leafcutter colonies have many needs that must be met. Some ants tend the fungus garden. Others bring leaves back to the nest. Others defend the nest and the queen ant. Leafcutter colonies have only one queen. The colony's queen is much larger than the other ants. The queen's job is to lay eggs. She can lay up to 30,000 eggs a day. Over her lifetime, a queen may lay as many as 50 million eggs.

Not all of these eggs are the same. The queen produces different types of eggs depending on the colony's needs. When a colony is new, the queen will produce gardener-nurse ants. These ants feed the newborn ants. They also take care of the queen's fungus garden. To do this, the gardener ants spread the fungus around. This helps the fungus grow more quickly.

As the nest grows, the queen will lay eggs for worker ants called foragers. These ants find, cut, and haul leaf pieces back to the nest. Another type of worker ant is called a within-nest specialist. These ants help clean the nest and rebuild the fungus garden. They help turn leaves into food for the fungus gardens. They also dig vents that bring air into the nest.

GLOSSARY A glossary might give one of these meanings for *offspring*:
1. Progeny or descendants;
2. A result or product. Which meaning of *offspring* best fits the way the word is used on this page? Why?

10   Like most animals, leafcutter ants have predators. When a nest has grown to a fairly large size, the queen begins to produce soldier ants. These soldiers defend the nest from predators and rival ant colonies. Soldier ants are the largest of the queen's offspring, or children. They have razor-sharp teeth to help them protect the colony.

The Value of Leafcutter Ants

CAUSE AND EFFECT
Although many people think leafcutter ants are pests, the writer states that they are valuable. What causes the writer to make this claim?

Many people consider leafcutter ants to be pests because of the damage they cause to plants. These ants often destroy gardens and crops. They can strip a large tree of all its leaves in one day. However, leafcutter ants are an important part of a forest's ecosystem. They help spread important nutrients across a forest. The tunnels and vents they dig also bring air into the forest's soil and keep it fertile. They are a valuable part of the forest ecosystem.

Leafcutter ants are particularly important to another life form—the fungus that they grow. The ants take excellent care of the fungus. It receives a constant supply of food. The fungus is also kept safe from predators and free of disease because of the ants' efforts. In return, the fungus digests leaves, which the ants cannot do on their own. The ants obtain nutrients by eating the fungus but do not consume it all.

It is hard to believe that a tiny ant might have valuable lessons to share with humans. But people can learn many things from leafcutter ants. For instance, scientists are studying how leafcutter ants keep diseases from harming their fungus gardens. The methods that the ants use may help humans create better medicines. Leafcutter ants may have other secrets that could help improve our lives. We still have much to learn about these creatures that may be Earth's oldest farmers.

TRANSITION WORDS The word *also* connects similar ideas. Paragraph 12 states, "The fungus is also kept safe from predators and free of disease because of the ants' efforts." What similar idea does the word *also* connect this statement to?

The queen leafcutter ant is much larger than the other ants in the colony. She is about the size of your thumb. Leafcutter ants and the fungi that they grow benefit each other. Each performs tasks that the other cannot.

Comprehension Check

Look back at "Leafcutter Ants." How do the responsibilities vary among the different ants in a leafcutter ant colony? For each type of ant, provide one or two tasks for which this ant is responsible.

Type of Ant	Tasks
Queen	lays up to 50 million eggs
Gardener-nurse	
Forager	
Within-nest specialist	
Soldier	

Vocabulary

Use the word map below to help you define and use one of the highlighted vocabulary words from the Share and Learn selection you are about to read or another word you choose.

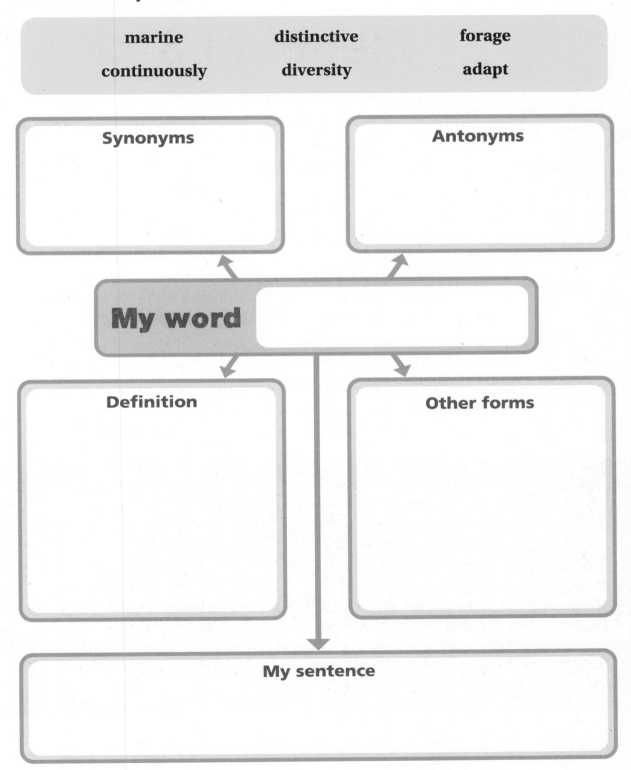

| marine | distinctive | forage |
| continuously | diversity | adapt |

Synonyms

Antonyms

My word

Definition

Other forms

My sentence

Consider ▶ How do elephant seal colonies differ from leafcutter ant colonies?

What similarities can you observe between these two creatures?

Elephant Seals

MAKE INFERENCES
Why do you think visitors to Año Nuevo State Park are led by a park ranger to view the elephant seals?

_____

_____

_____

1   For a sight worth seeing, travel fifty-five miles south of San Francisco, California, to Año Nuevo State Park. At the park, a ranger will lead you through grassy sand dunes. Past these dunes you can visit an enormous colony of northern elephant seals. But before you see these creatures, you will hear them—squealing, grunting, and trumpeting. They're noisy, and they are massive! Some elephant seals weigh over two tons. Their size is not the only reason they got their name, though. Like elephants, male elephant seals have big, bumpy trunks above their mouths. And if they are threatened, elephant seals can be dangerous.

Elephant seals belong to an animal group called pinnipeds (PIH-nuh-pehds). Pinnipeds are marine mammals with front and hind flippers. These animals breathe air like humans and other mammals. However, they live most of their lives in the water. Seals, sea lions, and walruses are in this group.

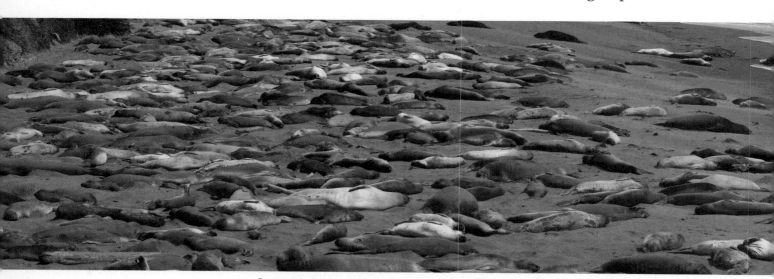

Several times each year, thousands of northern elephant seals return to central California's beaches. These elephant seals are sleeping.

Male and female elephant seals differ greatly in size and appearance. Some people might even mistake males and females for different types of animals. Male elephant seals are called bulls. They might be ten times as large as females, which are known as cows. Males also have thicker skin on their necks, and only males have the distinctive trunks above their mouths. Males and females also behave differently. Because of their different sizes, they eat different types of food. Males eat fish and sharks, and females eat squid and other slippery creatures.

MAIN IDEA AND DETAILS On the lines below, write the main idea of paragraph 3. Then, underline two details in the text that support this main idea.

_____

_____

_____

A Life at Sea

There are two types of elephant seals—northern and southern. Northern elephant seals live in the North Pacific Ocean. They can be found from Alaska to Baja California, Mexico. These seals spend most of their lives in the open sea. In fact, northern seals spend the majority of their lives underwater. They eat, travel, and even sleep below the ocean's surface. Thick layers of fat, or blubber, help keep these seals warm in this cold, watery environment.

5   Southern elephant seals are even larger than northern seals. In fact, they are the largest of any type of seal. Male southern elephant seals also have larger trunks than northern elephant seals. Like northern seals, these seals spend most of their lives at sea. But southern elephant seals are found in the frigid waters near Antarctica. The sea temperature in these areas is very cold. However, these waters are full of fish, squid, and other foods that the seals enjoy.

The largest of all pinnipeds, male southern elephant seals can weigh as much as 8,800 pounds.

CITE EVIDENCE The author does not directly say that elephant seals have special features that help them to find food in their environment, but this idea is implied in paragraph 6. What evidence from the paragraph can you cite to support this idea? Underline two details that provide this evidence.

PARAPHRASE In your own words, restate the last sentence of paragraph 7.

_____

_____

_____

CAUSE AND EFFECT Elephant seals have the ability to dive to great depths for long periods of time. Underline four special qualities that allow them this ability.

Both northern and southern elephant seals swim thousands of miles every year. They often dive to great depths, where the ocean is very dark. Some types of marine life, such as squid and octopuses, glow in the dark. This helps elephant seals find them in dark waters. They use their large eyes to find their prey. They also use their stiff whiskers to "feel" for food. Thousands of feet below the surface, they find fish, crabs, rays, and some small sharks.

Expert Divers

Elephant seals can dive to depths of 5,000 feet. That is nearly a mile below the surface! They can also remain underwater for up to two hours. When they do surface, they need only three to five minutes to breathe before diving again. The pressure of the water at these depths is far too great for humans to survive. In fact, elephant seals' diving abilities exceed those of almost all mammals, including most whales.

Usually, elephant seals do not reach these record depths. A male elephant seal will typically dive for about thirty minutes. Females usually spend slightly less time below the surface. But females often dive deeper than the male seals in search of food. They normally reach depths of 1,500 to 2,500 feet. Few other predators reach these depths to hunt or forage. This means the seals are able to find large amounts of food at these depths.

To survive the harsh conditions at such great depths, elephant seals have special qualities. Unlike humans, they empty their lungs of air before diving. They hold most of the oxygen they need in their blood instead of in their lungs. They also compress their layers of fatty blubber. This allows them to quickly sink far below the surface. While diving, a seal will slow down its heart rate to only four to fifteen beats per minute. The seal's blood flows only to its brain and other important organs. This helps keep the seal warm in the frigid ocean depths. In addition, elephant seals can still function when most of their oxygen is used up. This allows them to remain underwater for longer than almost any other mammal.

Elephant Seal Migrations

10   On shore, elephant seals form enormous colonies like the one at Año Nuevo State Park. However, they spend months alone at sea. Most mammals that migrate only make the journey once a year. Northern elephant seals are unusual because they migrate twice a year.

In early spring, elephant seals leave their beaches in the south. They all head north. However, the males swim along the continental shelf, and the females travel north through deeper waters farther away from the shore. These are the routes where they can find the most food. While migrating, the seals eat continuously. They rarely even pause to sleep. This nonstop eating helps them build up the layer of blubber that protects them from the cold. The blubber will also sustain the seals when they return to shore. Instead of eating while on shore, they will live from the energy stored in their blubber.

Male northern elephant seals travel more than 13,000 miles each year. They swim up the Pacific coast to the icy Gulf of Alaska and the Aleutian Islands. Then, they turn south and begin the journey back to California. Female northern elephant seals end their journey south of the Gulf of Alaska. Still, they swim more than 11,000 miles each year.

The female elephant seals are the first to arrive back at southern beaches in late spring. All the males arrive by the middle of the summer. At the end of the summer, the seals set off on their second migration of the year.

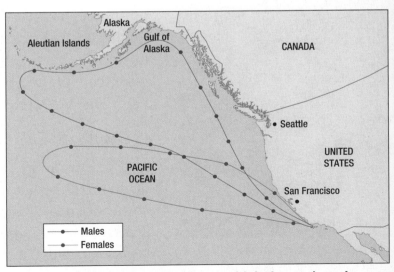

Because of the extreme depths at which the seals swim, humans rarely see elephant seals while they are migrating.

> **CONTEXT CLUES** What does continuously mean? Write your definition below. Underline the sections of the text that help you understand this word.
>
> _____
>
> _____
>
> _____

> **TRANSITION WORDS** Look at the last sentence in paragraph 12. Why does the writer begin the sentence with the word *still*?
>
> _____
>
> _____
>
> _____

These demonstrations of force help determine the leader in an elephant seal colony.

Life on Shore

After their travels, most elephant seals return to the beaches on which they were born. On shore, the seals mate and give birth. In winter, each adult female gives birth to one baby seal, called a pup. A pup weighs about 75 pounds at birth. But within one month it may weigh 250 to 350 pounds! In four to six weeks, pups learn to swim in rainwater ponds. Soon after, they're ready for the open sea.

15   Elephant seals also return to shore to molt each year. Molting is a process of shedding old skin and hair. The seals must do this on land. They would lose too much body heat if they molted in the water. While molting, elephant seals look ragged. But within four weeks, they have silvery new coats. Over the year, these coats fade to tan or brown. Then, it will be time to molt again.

An elephant seal's life on shore isn't always quiet. Bulls often fight for alpha, or leader, status. Some of these fights can be violent. The bulls rear up and slam their bodies against each other. Sometimes they fight with their sharp teeth. Sometimes the males just rear up without fighting. Then they throw back their heads and show off the size of their noses. This behavior can be enough to make an opponent back down.

Both male and female seals eat nothing while they are on shore. They rely on the thick blubber they have built up through the year to provide all of the energy they need during this fast. While fasting, the seals may lose as much as 40 percent of their body weight. They will gain this weight back when they return to sea.

Protecting Elephant Seals

By swimming at extreme depths, elephant seals can often avoid most predators. However, great white sharks are a common threat. Orcas, or killer whales, also feed on elephant seals. However, in the past, the greatest threat to elephant seals was neither sharks nor whales. It was humans.

Hundreds of thousands of elephant seals once lived in the Pacific Ocean. But in the 1800s, many people began hunting them for their blubber. This blubber was used to create fuel for lamps and other goods. By 1892, there were fewer than 100 northern elephant seals left. These remaining seals lived on an island off the coast of Baja California, Mexico. Then, the Mexican and U.S. governments began passing laws to protect the seals. The seal population began to grow again. Now there are about 160,000 of them.

20   The incredible survival of the northern elephant seal should be celebrated. However, the population is still at risk. Every northern elephant seal alive today came from the same few ancestors. This means that there is very little diversity among them. Because of this lack of variety, they are all vulnerable to the same diseases. As a result, one disease could wipe out a large number of the elephant seals.

Southern elephant seals have more diversity than northern elephant seals. They don't face the same threats. However, if ocean temperatures rise as a result of global warming, both northern and southern elephant seals may be threatened. Scientists have noticed that more male seals are born when waters are warmer. This may mean that the seals are adapting to a changing climate. But with more males than females, fewer babies will be born. Seal colonies will shrink.

PROBLEM AND SOLUTION What problem does the author say the seals faced in the 1800s? What was the solution to the problem?

_____

_____

_____

SUPPORTING DETAILS What detail supports the claim that there is very little diversity among northern elephant seals?

_____

_____

_____

Once a major danger to elephant seals, today people work to protect these remarkable creatures.

While seals sleep on the shore, scientists can easily attach satellite tags to the animals' foreheads.

Learning from Elephant Seals

Many scientists study elephant seals. They hope to find ways to protect the seals. Studying elephant seals may also improve medical treatments for humans. For instance, scientists want to learn how elephant seals survive with so little oxygen. When people suffer heart attacks or strokes, oxygen may not reach important organs. This can be very dangerous. Learning how elephant seals survive with little oxygen may help people recover from these life-threatening events.

Humans also can learn a thing or two from elephant seals' incredible diving skills. Even with special gear, humans cannot dive nearly as deep as elephant seals. The water pressure at these great depths is even too strong for remote-controlled vehicles. To understand conditions in these deep waters, scientists attach satellite tags to elephant seals. As seals dive deep below the surface, the tags record information. When the seals come to shore, the information is sent to a satellite. Scientists can then access the information from their labs. The tags are glued to the seals' foreheads. That way, they fall off when the seals molt each spring.

The tags also help scientists understand the routes that seals follow each year. They record information about the water's depth. They also measure the water's temperature and salt content. As this information changes from year to year, scientists can find out how the seals adapt to these changes. Hopefully, this research will help make sure elephant seals are around for a long time.

Anchor Standard Discussion Questions

Discuss the following questions with your peer group. Then record your answers in the space provided.

1. "Elephant Seals" describes ways in which scientists study elephant seals. Who do you think benefits more from these studies, elephant seals or humans? Why? Support your answer with details from the text.

_____

_____

_____

_____

_____

_____

2. Every text has a tone, even a work of scientific nonfiction. What is the tone of the article "Elephant Seals"? Support your answer with specific words and phrases from the text.

_____

_____

_____

_____

_____

Comprehension Check

1. The writer discusses several threats to the elephant seal population. Which threat do you think is the greatest? What evidence from the article supports this inference?

   _____

   _____

   _____

2. How might studying elephant seals improve life for human beings? Use evidence from the selection to support your answer.

   _____

   _____

   _____

3. What specialized features does the author describe that enable elephant seals to survive in their environment?

   _____

   _____

   _____

Read On Your Own

Read another scientific nonfiction text, "The Record Holders," independently. Apply what you learned in this lesson and check your understanding.

Writing Opinion Pieces

With the click of a mouse, a world of online information is at our fingertips. But not everyone has computer skills. Many people, especially the elderly, need training in how to use online resources.

Could you persuade your local library to offer computer courses for older patrons? How could you do that? One way would be to write a persuasive letter.

ESSENTIAL QUESTION

What makes an opinion piece effective?

What's an Opinion Piece?

How many printed books are in your classroom? How many electronic books are there? In classrooms of the future, do you think printed books will disappear? Do you think electronic texts of all sorts can make us smarter and better informed? Or do you think that printed books will always be an essential part of education and learning? What is your opinion?

In an **opinion piece**, you tell about your opinion and try to persuade others to agree with you. The flow chart below describes some ways to make your opinion piece effective.

Your Opinion
State your opinion clearly. It should tell your readers exactly how you feel about a topic.

Supporting Reasons
Include at least three reasons that support your opinion. Supporting reasons can include judgments and facts. Strong supporting reasons will make your opinion piece more convincing.

A Conclusion
Your conclusion sums up your ideas and completes your opinion piece.

Let's look at an opinion piece.

Analyze a Mentor Text

This is an example of an effective fifth-grade opinion piece. Read the letter and then complete the activities in the boxes as a class.

Computer Training for All

Dear Mr. Chang,

Every Saturday morning, I volunteer in the children's room at the library. The library is always busy then, especially in the computer center. However, most of the people using the computers are teenagers. Some elderly people do not feel comfortable there because they lack computer skills. The library should provide instruction in basic computer and Internet skills for older library patrons.

First of all, computer classes would help seniors find information more quickly. They could use digital almanacs and online dictionaries, like *The American Heritage Dictionary*. They would learn how to locate, bookmark, and download reliable information on the Internet. For example, the Internet Public Library has hundreds of links. The National Institutes of Health has an online encyclopedia of health topics. Sites like Project Gutenberg and the Online Books Page have thousands of free classics, from poems like "Casey at the Bat" to novels like *Oliver Twist*.

Second, computer competence would make life easier for older people. For example, elders would find it convenient to order groceries online, find an electrician, or make travel plans. They could learn to use the library's Web site and electronic card catalog and could access the library from home. They could reserve and put a hold on a book. Furthermore, they could find out about special library events. Internet competence is especially important for older patrons who are disabled or who may find it difficult to reach books on the shelves.

OPINION In the introduction, the writer gets the reader's attention by telling about a personal experience. The writer also states an opinion about providing computer classes. Circle the writer's opinion.

SUPPORTING REASONS The writer gives reasons that support his opinion in the second and third paragraphs. Underline the reason in each paragraph.

Finally, computer classes would bring old and young people together and make life more fun. Grandparents would be able to e-mail their grandchildren. They could play computer games or watch videos together. Teenage volunteers could teach the computer classes. With training, some of them would be excellent computer instructors. Teens might even earn course credits in exchange for teaching a class.

In conclusion, our elders need access to the knowledge available on the Internet. They also deserve the convenience and fun of using it. The library computer center is for everyone, not just for teenagers but also for older patrons. The twenty-first century has been called the Information Age. However, it is not a true Information Age unless everyone has access to computers and knows how to use them.

Sincerely,

Marco Gomez

Think About It ▶ What personal experience did the author draw on when planning this opinion piece?

Do you think the reader is likely to be persuaded by the opinion piece? Why or why not?

Vocabulary Study: Latin Roots and Affixes

A **root** is a word or word part that carries the core meaning of a word. A word's meaning can be changed by adding beginnings or endings called **affixes**. A **prefix** is an affix attached to the beginning of a word. A **suffix** is an affix attached to the end of a word. Many English roots and affixes come from Latin. The chart below identifies some common Latin prefixes, suffixes, and roots. Work with your class or a partner to fill the blank boxes with words using each prefix, suffix, or root.

Prefix	Root	Word
re- (again)	claim (to assert ownership)	reclaim
dis- (not, opposite of)	appear (to come into view)	
inter- (between)	library (a place to read or borrow books)	

Root	Suffix	Word
port (to carry)	-able (can be done)	portable
insist (to demand)	-ence (state, condition)	
act (to do)	-ion (process)	

Look back at the opinion piece on pages 237 and 238. Find one word with a prefix and one with a suffix, and complete the chart below. Use a dictionary to check the word meanings. Then write your own sentences using the words.

Word
Prefix
Meaning
Sentence

Word
Suffix
Meaning
Sentence

Writing Process

Now that you have read and analyzed an opinion piece, you are going to create your own by following these steps of the writing process.

1. Get Ready: Brainstorm List several topics you might want to write about. Choose the topic that you have the strongest opinion about.

2. Organize Use a graphic organizer to organize and plan your opinion piece.

3. Draft Create the first draft of your opinion piece. Focus on getting your ideas down.

4. Peer Review Work with a partner to evaluate and improve your draft.

5. Revise Use suggestions from your peer review to revise your opinion piece.

6. Edit Check your work carefully for spelling, punctuation, and grammar errors.

7. Publish Create a final version of your opinion piece.

Writing Assignment

In this lesson, you will write your own opinion piece. As you create this piece, remember the elements of the mentor text that were most effective. Read the following assignment.

Some people feel that printed books will one day be a thing of the past. They believe that in the future, all books will be electronic, read on computer screens and electronic devices. Are printed books in danger of disappearing? Will they someday belong only in museums? Would that be a good thing or not?

Write five paragraphs stating your opinion about whether or not printed books should be replaced with electronic books. Include research about the cost, benefits, and effectiveness of both. Be persuasive!

1. Get Ready: Brainstorm a Topic

The first step in writing an opinion piece is to choose your topic and opinion. Begin by listing several topics about electronic texts that you have strong opinions about. For each one, write your opinion about that topic.

Here's how the author of the mentor opinion piece brainstormed topics.

Classroom Web site	Electronic textbooks	Computer classes
Getting class assignments while at home is more convenient.	E-textbooks are less expensive and more convenient than print textbooks.	The library should offer classes in basic computer skills for older people.

Try It!   Use a Brainstorming Graphic Organizer

Now use the chart below to help brainstorm topics for your own opinion piece. Choose the aspect of printed versus electronic texts that you feel most strongly about.

Brainstorm Ideas for Your Topic

You can use a graphic organizer to help brainstorm ideas and details for your opinion piece. Here is how the author of the mentor text used the graphic organizer.

OPINION Begin by stating your opinion clearly and strongly.

REASONS Give reasons that support your opinion. You may add to or revise your reasons as you draft your opinion piece.

DETAILS Now is the time to think of details that help explain your reasons. You will probably think of more details as you draft your opinion piece.

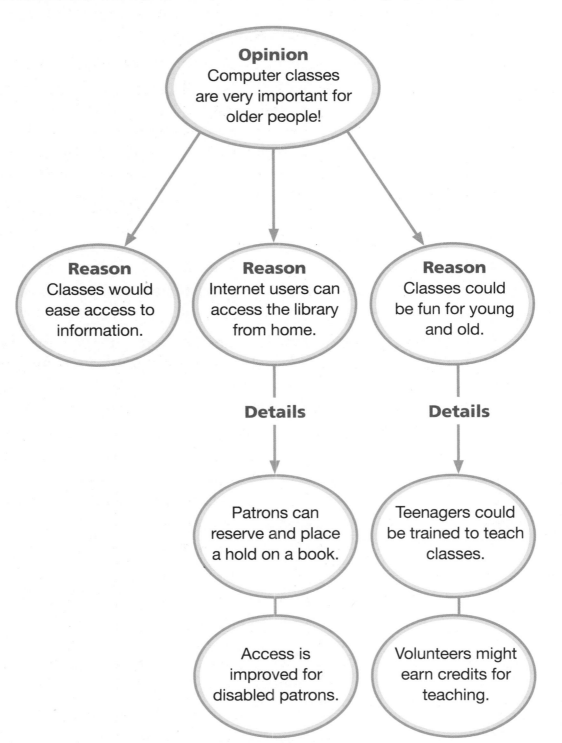

Opinion
Computer classes are very important for older people!

Reason
Classes would ease access to information.

Reason
Internet users can access the library from home.

Reason
Classes could be fun for young and old.

Details

Details

Patrons can reserve and place a hold on a book.

Teenagers could be trained to teach classes.

Access is improved for disabled patrons.

Volunteers might earn credits for teaching.

Try It!

Use a Graphic Organizer to Get Started

Now use the idea web below to brainstorm your opinion, reasons, and details for your own opinion piece.

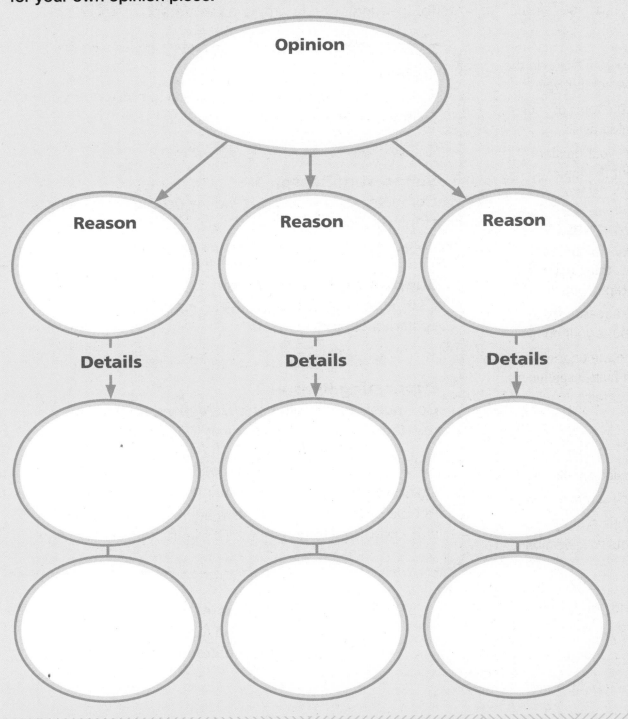

2. Organize

You are almost ready to begin a draft of your opinion piece. You can use a graphic organizer to help organize the ideas and details you gathered during brainstorming. You can then refer to the graphic organizer as you work through the different parts of your draft. The writer of the mentor text completed this graphic organizer.

INTRODUCTION In the first paragraph, you

- tell the topic of your opinion piece
- state your opinion about the topic

SUPPORTING PARAGRAPHS In the second, third, and fourth paragraphs, you

- give a reason that supports your opinion
- elaborate on the reason with facts, experiences, and details

CONCLUSION Your conclusion should

- briefly summarize your reasons
- restate your opinion

Opinion
The library should provide instruction in basic computer skills for elderly people.

Supporting Reason 1
Computer skills would give elderly people easier access to information.

Supporting Reason 2
Computer skills and Internet access would make life easier for seniors.

Supporting Reason 3
Computer skills could bring old and young people together. Teenagers could teach the classes.

Conclusion
People of all ages should have access to computers and know how to use them. This is the Information Age.

Try It! **Organize Your Opinion Piece**

Now use the graphic organizer below to organize the ideas and details you want to use in the different paragraphs of the draft of your opinion piece.

Opinion

Supporting Reason 1

Supporting Reason 2

Supporting Reason 3

Conclusion

3. Draft

Now it is time to begin the first draft of your opinion piece. Remember, your draft does not have to be perfect! This is the time to use your notes, get your ideas down in some sort of organized way, and have fun. You will have time to revise your writing later. Start by drafting your opinion paragraphs on a computer or on a separate sheet of paper. Tell your opinion about printed versus electronic texts.

Writer's Craft: Using Linking Words and Phrases

Linking words and phrases help writing flow smoothly. They also help readers understand how opinions and reasons are connected. Here are some common linking words and phrases.

Linking words	although, because, before, consequently, first, furthermore, finally, nevertheless, specifically, then, therefore
Linking phrases	even though, as long as, in addition, in spite of, the first reason, for example, most important, with reference to

The author of the mentor text uses linking words and phrases in his third paragraph.

LINKING WORDS AND PHRASES
Read this section of the mentor text. Circle the linking words and phrases. Underline an example of how computer competence makes life easier for older patrons.

Second, computer competence would make life easier for older people. For example, elders would find it convenient to order groceries online, find an electrician, or make travel plans. They could learn to use the library's Web site and electronic card catalog and could access the library from home. They could reserve and put a hold on a book. Furthermore, they could find out about special library events. Internet competence is especially important for older patrons who are disabled or who may find it difficult to reach books on the shelves.

Try It! **Write Your First Draft**

On a computer or a separate sheet of paper, continue the draft of your opinion piece. Remember to use linking words and phrases to connect your ideas. Use this drafting checklist to help you as you write.

✔ A good beginning gets your reader's attention. You can begin with a question, a quotation, or an interesting or funny experience.

✔ Be sure to state your opinion in the first paragraph.

✔ Write a topic sentence that clearly states the reason in each supporting paragraph.

✔ Use the reasons and details you wrote during Step 2: Organize.

✔ In each supporting paragraph, include sentences with details, facts, and experiences.

✔ Connect your ideas with linking words and phrases.

✔ Summarize your reasons in the end. Try to write an ending that your readers will remember.

Tips for Writing Your First Draft

- Talk to a classmate about your topic. The classmate might have some suggestions to help you get started.

- Focus on ideas, not details. Since you will revise and edit later, you can fix the details then. In drafting, it's the ideas that count.

- If you get stuck, take a walk around the block. Physical activity can help to jump-start your brain!

4. Peer Review

After you finish your draft, you can work with a partner to review each other's drafts. Here is a draft of the mentor text. Read it with your partner. Together, answer the questions in the boxes. Then we'll see how the writer's classmate evaluated the draft.

An Early Draft:

INTRODUCTION In his draft, the writer does not state his opinion clearly. Does he plan to focus on computer classes for elderly people or on getting more computers for the library?

SUPPORTING PARAGRAPHS The third paragraph could use some linking words and phrases to make the ideas clearer. Which linking word or phrase could you add to the first sentence? What phrase could you add to the beginning of the third sentence?

CONCLUSION The conclusion does not summarize the writer's reasons. How would you sum up the writer's reasons?

Computers for All!

As a library volunteer, I've noticed that most people using the computers at the library are teenagers. Maybe that's because teens have a lot of homework. Many elderly people do not feel comfortable there because they lack computer skills. Also there are not enough computers at the library.

Computer skills would make it easier for elderly people to find information. They would be able to look up information and feel more connected. Some sites have hundreds of links and are easy to navigate.

Computers make life easier. Elders could learn how to do lots of things online. They could learn to use the library's Web site and electronic card catalog and could access the library from home. They could reserve and put a hold on a book. They could find out about special library events. At-home library access is especially convenient for older patrons who are disabled.

Computer skills would make life more fun by bringing old and young people together. For example, grandparents would be able to e-mail their grandchildren or play computer games with them. Teenage volunteers might teach the computer classes. With training, some teens would be excellent computer instructors.

In conclusion, I want to emphasize that everyone should be able to use computers.

An Example Peer Review Form

This peer review form gives an example of how a classmate evaluated the draft of the mentor text shown on the previous page.

The introduction states the topic in an interesting way.	You did a good job of *telling the reader about your experiences volunteering at the library.*
The writer gives a clear, strong opinion statement.	You could improve your opinion piece by *writing one strong opinion statement. You have two opinions in the introduction.*

The writer supports the opinion with at least three strong reasons.	You did a good job of *giving three reasons.*
The writer uses interesting details to explain the reasons.	You could improve your opinion piece by *adding more details to the second paragraph to support the idea that learning computer skills would help elders.*

The writer uses linking words and phrases to make the writing flow smoothly.	You did a good job of *using "In conclusion" in the last paragraph.*
	You could improve your opinion piece by *adding linking phrases such as "Another reason" and "For example" in the third paragraph.*

The conclusion sums up the supporting reasons.	You did a good job of *restating your opinion.*
	You could improve your opinion piece by *adding a sentence that summarizes your three reasons.*

Try It! Peer Review with a Partner

Now you are going to work with a partner to review each other's opinion piece drafts. You will use the peer review form below. If you need help, look back at the mentor text writer's peer review form for suggestions.

The introduction states the topic in an interesting way. **The writer gives a clear, strong opinion statement.**	You did a good job of --- You could improve your opinion piece by
The writer supports the opinion with three strong reasons. **The writer uses interesting details to explain the reasons.**	You did a good job of --- You could improve your opinion piece by
The writer uses linking words and phrases to make the writing flow smoothly.	You did a good job of --- You could improve your opinion piece by
The conclusion sums up the supporting reasons.	You did a good job of --- You could improve your opinion piece by

Try It! Record Key Peer Review Comments

Now it's time for you and your partner to share your comments with each other. Listen to your partner's feedback, and write down the key comments in the left column. Then write some ideas for improving your draft in the right column.

My review says that my introduction	I will
My review says that my reasons	I will
My review says that my use of details	I will
My review says that my use of linking words	I will
My review says that my conclusion	I will

Use the space below to write anything else you notice about your draft that you think you can improve.

5. Revise

In this step of the writing process, you work on parts of your draft that need improvement. Use the peer review form that your classmate completed to help you. You can also use your own ideas about how to improve each part of your opinion piece. This checklist includes some things to think about as you get ready to revise.

Revision Checklist

✓ Does my beginning catch the reader's interest? Do I state my opinion clearly?

✓ Do my reasons support my opinion in a strong way?

✓ Do I use details to make my reasons clear and strong?

✓ Do I use linking words to make the writing flow smoothly?

✓ Is my conclusion interesting? Have I summed up my reasons well?

Writer's Craft: Using Correlative Conjunctions

Conjunctions are words that join together two parts of a sentence. Some common conjunctions are *and*, *but*, *so*, *or*, *nor*, *yet*, *because*, *since*, *unless*, and *although*. **Correlative conjunctions** are two conjunctions that relate to each other. They join two ideas in a sentence and can make an opinion piece more convincing. These are some common correlative conjunctions: *both ... and*; *not ... but*; *either ... or*; *not only ... but also*; *not just ... but also*; *neither ... nor*.

CORRELATIVE CONJUNCTIONS Find the sentence with correlative conjunctions in this paragraph. Underline the sentence.

Try writing the sentence in another way here.

_____

_____

In conclusion, our elders need access to the knowledge available on the Internet. They also deserve the convenience and fun of using it. The library computer center is for everyone, not just for teenagers but also for older patrons. The twenty-first century has been called the Information Age. However, it is not a true Information Age unless everyone has access to computers and knows how to use them.

Try It! Revise Your Opinion Piece

Practice using correlative conjunctions. Replace the short sentences below with one sentence that contains correlative conjunctions. Use the correlative conjunctions suggested for each sentence.

1. Printed books are beautiful to look at. They are also beautiful to hold. (both … and)

   _____

2. My mother does not have an e-reader. My father also doesn't have one. (neither … nor)

   _____

3. My mom is going to give my dad an e-reader for his birthday. Or she might give it to him on their wedding anniversary. (either … or)

   _____

4. Electronic readers are practical in a small apartment. They are also practical on an airplane. (not only … but also)

   _____

Writing Assignment

Now it's time to revise the draft of your opinion piece. Continue working on a computer or on a separate sheet of paper. Review the assignment, repeated below, and the checklist. Make sure you have included everything you need!

> Some people feel that printed books will one day be a thing of the past. They believe that in the future, all books will be electronic, read on computer screens and electronic devices. Are printed books in danger of disappearing? Will they someday belong only in museums? Would that be a good thing or not?
>
> Write five paragraphs stating your opinion about whether or not printed books should be replaced with electronic books. Include research about the cost, benefits, and effectiveness of both. Be persuasive!

6. Edit

After revising your opinion piece, you will edit it. When you edit, you read very carefully to find any mistakes. Here's a checklist of some things to look for.

Editing Checklist

✓ Did you indent each paragraph?

✓ Are all of your sentences complete? Does each have a subject and a verb?

✓ Did you begin each sentence with a capital letter?

✓ Does each sentence end with the correct punctuation?

✓ Have you used commas correctly?

✓ Are all of your words spelled correctly?

You can use these editing marks to mark any errors you find.

^ Add   ~~delete~~ Delete   ↱ Insert comma

⊔⊓ Reverse the order

This paragraph from an early draft of the mentor text shows how to use editing marks.

> Computer skills would make life more fun by bringing old and young people together. For example‸ grandparents
>
> *their*
> would be able to e-mail ~~there~~ grandchildren or play computer games with them. Teenage volunteers might
>
> *teach*
> ~~teech~~ the computer classes. With training‸ some teens would be excellent instructors‿computer.

Language Focus: Using Punctuation to Clarify

Using Commas in a Series

When three or more items are listed in a sentence, be sure to separate them with commas. Look at these examples:

- You can often find needed information in a dictionary, an encyclopedia, or an almanac.
- Our elders deserve the information, convenience, and fun of using the Internet.

Using Commas after a Linking Word or Phrase

When a linking word or phrase begins a sentence, separate it from the rest of the sentence with a comma. Look at these examples:

- Most important, printed books last longer.
- Consequently, e-books are here to stay.

Formatting Titles Correctly

Titles of large texts, like books and reference works, are italicized or underlined. Titles of shorter texts, like poems, magazine articles, songs, and short stories, are put in quotation marks.

> **Books, Plays, Large Texts:** *Romeo and Juliet* (play); *Tom Sawyer* (novel)
>
> **Poems, Short Stories, Songs:** "O Captain, My Captain" (poem); "Eleven" (short story)

First of all computer classes would help seniors find information more quickly. They could use digital almanacs and online dictionaries like The American Heritage Dictionary. They would learn how to locate bookmark and download reliable information on the Internet. For example the Internet Public Library has hundreds of links. The National Institutes of Health has an online encyclopedia of health topics. Sites like Project Gutenberg and the Online Books Page have thousands of free classics, from poems like Casey at the Bat to novels like Oliver Twist.

CORRECT PUNCTUATION
Read this paragraph from the mentor text. Use the information on this page to add any missing commas and format the titles correctly.

Try It! Language and Editing Practice

Correct the punctuation in the sentences below. Add any missing commas. Format titles correctly.

1. For example Merriam-Webster's Dictionary is a reliable reference source.

2. The following novels are available as e-books: Brian's Winter This Side of the Mountain and The Birchbark House.

3. I went to the library after school worked in the computer room and read for a while.

4. In addition books articles music and videos are available online.

5. For example the folk song This Land Is Your Land is available online.

Now use editing marks to correct the errors in this paragraph.

Many books poems musical compositions and historical documents are available on the Internet. For example you can find Lewis Carroll's books famous Alice in Wonderland and Through the Looking Glass, or songs such as our national anthem The Star Star Spangled Spangled Banner.

Try It! Edit Your Opinion Piece

Now edit your opinion piece. Use this checklist and the editing marks you have learned to correct any errors you find.

- ☐ Did you indent each paragraph?

- ☐ Are all of your sentences complete? Does each have a subject and a verb?

- ☐ Did you begin each sentence with a capital letter?

- ☐ Does each sentence end with the correct punctuation?

- ☐ Have you used commas correctly?

- ☐ Are all of your words spelled correctly?

- ☐ Have you punctuated book and Web site titles correctly?

Editing Tips

- Read your writing aloud. This will help you discover missing words and awkward phrases. Ask yourself, "Did that sound right?"

- Listen carefully as you read for stops and pauses. Stops and pauses usually indicate the places where punctuation might go. Ask yourself, "Have I missed any punctuation? Are titles formatted correctly?"

- Read your writing over at a slow pace at least two times. When reading for small details, one reading is not enough!

7. Publish

On a computer or a separate sheet of paper, create a neat final draft of your opinion piece. Correct all errors that you identified while editing your draft. Be sure to give your opinion piece an interesting title.

The final step is to publish your opinion piece. Here are some different ways you might choose to share your work.

- Read aloud your opinion piece to your class or to a small group of your classmates.

- Gather your opinion piece and the work of your classmates into a booklet.

- Create a bulletin board display with the class opinion pieces.

- Create a poster using your opinion piece and drawings or photographs from magazines.

- Write a letter to the editor of the local newspaper.

Technology Suggestions

- Upload your opinion piece onto your class or school blog.
- Print your opinion piece using decorative borders or paper.

Writing Handbook

A Guide to Functional Texts

Functional texts are things you read and write to help you in your day-to-day life. If you need to cook something, you read the recipe first. If you are going to a special event, you read the invitation to find out when and where the event will be. If you plan a party, you write invitations with the details. In this section, you will find examples of different functional texts and labels that show you the important features of each text. If you are asked to read or write one of these functional texts, use the sample in this handbook as a model to follow.

Models

On the top left-hand corner of the envelope, write your name, street address, city, state, and zip code.

Put a stamp on the top right-hand corner of the envelope.

Sender's Name
Street Address
City, State Zip Code

Recipient's Name
Street Address
City, State Zip Code

In the middle of the envelope, write the recipient's name, street address, city, state, and zip code.

Scott Mester
12 White Knoll Drive
Pleasantville, NY 12345

Carolyn Long
34 Church Road
Old Bridge, Michigan 45678

Write your address at the top of the letter.

347 Elm Street
Baton Rouge, LA 70801

Include the address of the person to whom you are sending the letter.

Include the date.

March 4, 2012

Mr. Frederick Wright
959 Canal Street
New Orleans, LA 70111

Address the person you are writing with a formal greeting, including any appropriate titles, such as "Mr." or "Ms."

Dear Mr. Wright:

The body paragraphs of your letter should be well organized and clear. Be sure to maintain a formal tone.

Thank you for responding to my letter. I have not had a chance to read your new book. It will have to wait until school is over. Thank you for answering my questions. Your answers were very helpful. I received an "A" on my assignment. My teacher said she was impressed. She had never seen so many facts and information about your book.

My new assignment is about jungle cats. My teacher gave us a list of topics to research. I chose jungle cats. I read different sources in the library. They gave me a lot of information about jungle cats. You mentioned that you went to Africa in your last letter. Did you see any jungle cats?

Remember that your closing should match the overall tone of the rest of the letter. "Regards" and "Sincerely" are good choices.

Sincerely,
Andrew Walker
Andrew Walker

Sign your letter. Under your signature, type your first and last name so there will be no confusion about the spelling of your name.

Write your address at the top of the letter. Include the date.

582 Elm Street
Springfield, MA, 01152
January 5, 2012

The greeting should say "hello" to the person to whom you are writing. A comma should follow the greeting.

Hi Veronica,

    What's up? How are you? I'm so glad you came out to visit last month. My mom says hi. Next time, I want to visit you. I've never been to New York. It sounds so fun. I want to go to the museums. I also want to see a musical. You're so lucky!

The body of the letter contains the main text or message. Each paragraph should be indented.

    I know we haven't talked in a while. I've been so, so busy with school. Mrs. Nelson gave us such a hard assignment. I've been living in the library. I have to look for so many sources. And all I can write are facts and examples. Can you imagine?

    Well, sorry I can't write a longer letter, but I have to get back to the library. I hope you are well.

The closing should say "good-bye." A comma follows the closing.

Your friend,

Sara

Sara

Sign your letter.

Start by providing the reason for the event.

Bill Cashman is celebrating his tenth birthday!

* 10 *

Join us as we celebrate on
Saturday, May 19, 2012 at 2:00 p.m.

Funtown Arcade
22 Middle Road
Springtown, Oregon

Regrets only to Mr. and Mrs. Cashman (123) 456-7890.

Include the date and time of the event.

Provide the location's name and address.

Provide a way for your guests to respond to the invitation.

Hello Mr. Dockery,

Please excuse Kevin from school for the week of November 12 to November 16. He has been diagnosed with chicken pox, and his doctor has recommended that he stay home to rest during his recovery.

Please send any available homework that he can complete during his illness, and Kevin will make up any work that he has missed when he returns to class.

Best,

Robyn Sayre

Robyn Sayre

Peanut Soup

Ingredients:

- ¼ cup unsalted butter
- 1 medium onion, finely chopped
- 2 celery stalks, finely chopped
- 3 tablespoons flour
- 8 cups chicken stock
- 2 cups creamy peanut butter
- 1 ¾ cups light cream
- salted peanuts, chopped

Instructions:

1. Chop the onion, celery, and peanuts separately and place them in individual bowls while you melt the butter in a saucepan over medium heat.

2. Once the butter is melted, add the onions and celery and cook for about 5 minutes, until softened. Stir often.

3. Stir in flour and cook for 2 minutes.

4. Increase heat and add chicken stock. After you bring mixture to a boil, reduce heat and cook until thickened (about 15 minutes).

5. Strain over a bowl. Squeeze the vegetables to contribute as much flavor to the soup as possible. Then pour the soup back into the saucepan.

6. Whisk the peanut butter and cream into the soup for about 5 minutes over low heat.

7. Garnish with peanuts and serve warm.

Yield: Makes about 10 servings.

> The title of the recipe tells you what dish you are preparing.

> The list of ingredients tells you what items you need to prepare the dish and how much of each item to use.

> The instructions tell you how to prepare the dish and what cooking methods you should use.

> The yield tells you how many servings the recipe will provide.

Crayon Blackout

Do you want something wonderful and exciting to do on a rainy day? If so, this is the perfect art project for you! When you first begin to make a crayon blackout, your artwork might not seem that interesting. But in the end, you will be surprised. You will have a beautiful work of art to brighten up any day.

Here is what you'll need:

- paper (computer paper or drawing paper)
- crayons
- newspaper
- popsicle sticks, forks, toothpicks, or combs
- tape (optional)

Here are the steps for creating a crayon blackout:

Step 1 Find a large, flat workspace, such as a table or the floor. Place sheets of newspaper over your whole work area.

Step 2 Pick out a piece of computer paper or drawing paper.

Step 3 Color all over your paper. Use as many colors of crayons as you like. Be sure to cover the entire piece of paper.

Step 4 Color over what you have done in black crayon. This can take a little time. Your hand might slip off the paper. That's OK! The newspaper is there to protect the floor or table. Take your time, and be sure to color your entire paper with black crayon.

Step 5 Scrape off parts of the black crayon to reveal the rainbow of colors underneath. To do this, pick a tool (a popsicle stick, a fork, a toothpick, or a comb). Scrape across your paper lightly. You want to take off only the black crayon. You want to leave the colorful crayon marks on your paper. Be careful not to tear your paper.

Step 6 Anywhere you scrape will reveal bright colors. So, use your imagination, and create wild designs!

Step 7 When you are done, you will have a rainbow of colors showing through the black crayon. You can use tape to hang your artwork on a window. When the rain ends, the bright sun will make your artwork glow!

How Hard or Soft?

All rocks are made up of a combination of two or more minerals. However, not all rocks are the same. Different rocks have different properties. A property is something you can observe. One property of a rock is its hardness, or how hard or soft it is. You can test for the hardness of a rock by following the instructions below.

1. Gather these materials:

   - glass plate
   - penny
   - nail
   - permanent marker
   - 4 different kinds of rocks
   - masking tape

2. Make a chart like this one:

Rock	Fingernail	Penny	Nail	Glass
A				
B				
C				
D				

3. Use the masking tape and marker to label the rocks A, B, C, and D.

4. Try to scratch each rock with your fingernail, the penny, and the nail. Were you able to leave a mark? Record your results on the chart by putting "yes" or "no" in each box.

5. Try to scratch the glass with each rock. Were you able to leave a mark? Record your results on the chart by putting "yes" or "no" in each box.

Which rocks were you able to scratch with your fingernail? Which rocks scratched the glass? Which rock is the hardest?

> List all the necessary steps in the experiment. Number them consecutively so the reader can easily follow the steps. Be sure they explain exactly how to perform the experiment and do not contain unnecessary information.

Provide a title at the top of the label.

If more information is needed, use an asterisk (*) and provide the additional information later.

List all items separately.

Remember to keep wording short. Space is limited, so only use the words that are needed.

Nutrition Facts
Serving Size 8 oz
Servings Per Container: About 3

Amount Per Serving

Calories 180   Calories from Fat 60

% Daily Value*

Total Fat 6g	10%
Saturated Fat 1g	5%
Trans Fat 0g	0%
Cholesterol 5mg	2%
Sodium 75mg	3%
Total Carbohydrate 26g	9%
Dietary Fiber 5g	19%
Sugars 11g	
Protein 8g	

Vitamin A 60%		Vitamin C 70%	
Calcium 8%		Iron 10%	

*Percent Daily Values are based on a 2,000 calorie diet. Your daily values may be higher or lower depending on your calorie needs.

	Calories	2,000	2,500
Total Fat	Less than	65g	80g
Sat Fat	Less than	20g	25g
Cholesterol	Less than	300mg	300mg
Sodium	Less than	2,400mg	2,400mg
Total Carbohydrate		300m	375g
Dietary Fiber		25g	30g

Calories per gram:

   Fat 9   Carbohydrate 4   Protein 4

The title of a time line will tell you what subjects the time line is explaining.

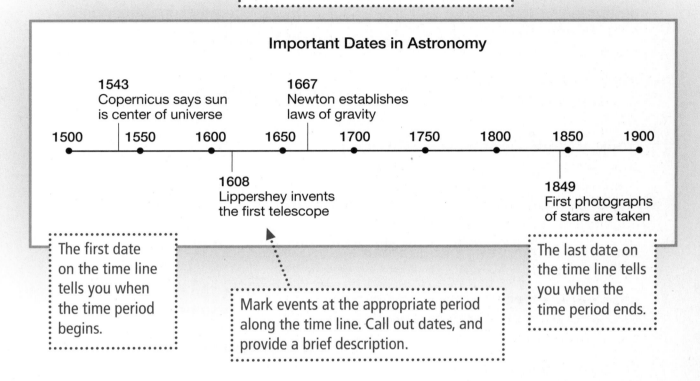

Important Dates in Astronomy

1543
Copernicus says sun is center of universe

1667
Newton establishes laws of gravity

1500 1550 1600 1650 1700 1750 1800 1850 1900

1608
Lippershey invents the first telescope

1849
First photographs of stars are taken

The first date on the time line tells you when the time period begins.

Mark events at the appropriate period along the time line. Call out dates, and provide a brief description.

The last date on the time line tells you when the time period ends.

Glossary

act a large section of a long drama, sometimes made up of scenes (Lesson 2)

affix a word part added to the beginning or ending of a word that changes the meaning of the word (Lesson 12)

antonym a word that has the opposite meaning of another word (Lesson 7)

body the middle of a piece of writing that gives more information about the main idea; the body of an essay comes between its introduction and its conclusion (Lesson 5)

cause something that brings about an effect or result (Lesson 11)

cause and effect the relationship that tells when one event causes another event to happen (Lesson 11)

chapter a section of a longer story (Lesson 1)

character a person, an animal, or an object that takes part in the action of a text (Lessons 1, 2, 3, 8, 10)

character traits details about a character's physical appearance or personality (Lesson 1)

chart a graphic organizer that uses columns and rows to organize information (Lessons 4, 6)

chronological order the order in which events happen (Lessons 4, 6, 7)

cite evidence to find information in a text that supports your thinking (Lessons 1, 2, 4, 6, 8, 9, 11)

climax the point in a fictional narrative when the conflict is the most serious; the high point of the action in a fictional narrative (Lesson 1)

comma a punctuation mark used to separate an introductory element from the rest of a sentence, to separate items in a series, to indicate direct address, or to set off a tag question or the words *yes* and *no* (Lessons 7, 12)

compare to show the similarities between two objects, ideas, people, places, or events (Lessons 2, 4, 10)

conclusion the ending of a piece of writing that sums up the text's main points and often leaves the reader with something to think about (Lessons 5, 10, 12)

conflict a problem that the main characters in a fictional narrative must face (Lesson 1)

conjunction a word that connects two words, sentences, or phrases, such as *and*, *but*, or *or* (Lessons 3, 12)

context clue a word or phrase in a text near an unknown word that gives clues about the meaning of the unknown word (Lessons 4, 6, 7, 8, 11)

contrast to show the differences between two objects, ideas, people, places, or events (Lessons 2, 4, 10)

correlative conjunctions two conjunctions that relate to each other and join two parts of a sentence, such as *both . . . and* (Lesson 12)

description specific information about a person, place, or thing (Lessons 3, 7)

details information in a fictional or personal narrative that tells who, what, when, where, or how (Lessons 3, 7); facts or ideas that tell about the main idea in a piece of writing (Lessons 5, 10, 11, 12)

diagram a drawing with labels that shows the different parts of an object or how something works (Lessons 5, 6)

dialect vocabulary and pronunciation that belong to a particular time, place, or social group (Lesson 10)

dialogue the words that characters speak in a text; a conversation between characters in a text (Lessons 3, 7)

dictionary a reference book in which words are listed alphabetically with their meanings, pronunciations, and other information (Lesson 5)

drama a story that is performed on a stage by actors; a play (Lesson 2)

effect a result of a cause (Lesson 11)

explanatory text see *informative text* (Lesson 5)

fictional narrative a story that the author makes up (Lesson 3)

figurative language language that does not mean exactly what it says; language that contains imagery or describes something through the use of unusual comparisons for added effect, interest, and meaning (Lessons 3, 8)

first-person point of view text in which the narrator is a character in the story and uses the pronoun *I* (Lesson 1)

flashback the narrative technique of leaving the present action of a fictional narrative to go back to events in the past (Lesson 3)

future perfect tense a verb tense that describes an action that will occur in the future before some other action, such as *will have gone* (Lesson 7)

genre a type of writing with a particular form or content, such as a short story, drama, or poem (Lesson 1)

glossary an alphabetical list of difficult or special words and their meanings that is usually printed at the end of a book (Lessons 4, 5, 11)

graphic features photographs, illustrations, time lines, diagrams, and graphs in a piece of nonfiction writing (Lesson 5)

graphic novel a genre of writing that uses both panels of illustrations and text to tell a story (Lesson 9)

historical nonfiction a genre of writing that tells about real events or people from the past (Lesson 4)

illustration a picture created by drawing or painting (Lesson 9)

informative text nonfiction text in which the author presents information about a specific subject and supports it with facts and details (Lesson 5)

integrate information to combine information from multiple sources to understand a topic more fully (Lesson 4)

interjection a word or phrase used in a way that shows feeling, such as *wow* or *oh* (Lesson 3)

introduction the beginning of a piece of writing that captures the reader's attention and presents the text's thesis statement, or main idea (Lessons 5, 12)

line a row of words; the basic building block of a poem (Lesson 8)

linking words and phrases words and phrases that connect ideas to make writing flow smoothly (Lessons 5, 10, 12)

literal language a word or phrase that means the same as its dictionary meaning (Lesson 8)

main idea the most important point in a piece of writing; what a text is mostly about (Lessons 4, 5, 10, 11)

make connections between texts to note the similarities and differences between texts, often in the same genre (Lesson 1)

make inferences to use information in the text and your own knowledge to figure out things that are not stated directly by the author (Lessons 2, 4, 6, 8, 9, 11)

map a visual representation of an area showing physical features, such as cities, roads, or rivers (Lesson 4)

metaphor a type of figurative language in which two unlike things are compared without using the word *like* or *as* (Lessons 3, 8)

narrative development the unfolding of a fictional narrative in which the conflict is developed through the events of the plot (Lesson 3)

narrator the person who tells a story (Lesson 1)

objective point of view a point of view in which the narrator presents the action and the characters' speech without comment or emotion and without revealing the characters' thoughts (Lesson 1)

opinion a personal belief that cannot be proved true (Lesson 12)

opinion piece a genre of writing in which the author states a personal belief and tries to persuade others to agree (Lesson 12)

pacing the act of controlling the pace, or rate of progress, of a fictional narrative (Lesson 3)

paraphrase to restate another person's writing or speech in your own words (Lessons 2, 4, 6, 8, 9, 11)

past perfect tense a verb tense that describes an action that happened in the past before some other event, such as *had gone* (Lesson 7)

personal narrative a genre of writing in which the author describes a personal experience (Lesson 7)

personification a type of figurative language in which something that is not human is given human qualities, such as feelings and actions (Lesson 3)

plot the series of events in a fictional narrative, narrative poem, or graphic novel that include the character's actions, a conflict, and a resolution (Lessons 1, 3, 8, 9)

poetry a genre of writing that is separated into lines and often stanzas in which an author uses descriptive language and sometimes sound devices, such as rhyme and rhythm, to create meaning and to produce an emotion in the reader (Lesson 8)

point of view the perspective from which a story is told; in the first-person point of view, one of the characters tells the story using the pronoun *I*; in the third-person point of view, a narrator uses the pronouns *he*, *she*, or *they* to tell the story (Lesson 1); an author's attitude about what he or she is describing in nonfiction text (Lesson 4)

precise language words and phrases that are clear, specific, and descriptive (Lessons 5, 10)

prefix an affix added to the beginning of a word that changes the meaning of the word (Lesson 12)

preposition a word that links a noun or pronoun to other words in a sentence, often to indicate how things are related in time or space (Lesson 3)

present perfect tense a verb tense that describes an action that began at an indefinite time in the past, such as *have gone* (Lesson 7)

problem a difficulty that a character must solve or overcome (Lesson 3)

problem and solution a method of organizing writing by stating a problem and describing its solution (Lesson 11)

resolution the conclusion of a story; the part of the plot that takes place after the climax, when the conflict has been resolved (Lessons 1, 3)

response to literature a genre of writing in which the author describes and analyzes some aspect of a literary work (Lesson 10)

rising action the growing seriousness of a conflict in a story (Lesson 1)

root word the base, or main part, of a word that carries its core meaning (Lesson 12)

scene a small section of a drama (Lesson 2)

scientific nonfiction nonfiction text that provides factual information about an area of science (Lesson 11)

sensory language language that appeals to a reader's sense of sight, hearing, taste, smell, or touch (Lesson 3)

sentence style the length and organization of a sentence (Lesson 5)

sequence of events the order in which events happen (Lessons 1, 2, 7)

setting the time and place when and where a story happens (Lessons 3, 7, 8, 10)

short story a fictional narrative with characters, a setting, and a plot that is usually short enough to read in one sitting (Lesson 1)

simile a type of figurative language in which two unlike things are compared using the word *like* or *as* (Lessons 3, 8)

source a book, Web site, or other reference material that you consult while doing research (Lesson 5)

stanza a series of lines that makes up a section of a poem (Lesson 8)

suffix an affix added to the end of a word that changes the meaning of the word (Lesson 12)

summarize to retell the main points or plot of a text in your own words (Lessons 2, 4, 7, 8, 9, 11)

supporting details facts or other information that back up an author's main idea in a piece of nonfiction writing (Lessons 4, 5, 7, 11)

supporting paragraphs paragraphs in nonfiction text that elaborate on the topic with explanations, supporting details, and facts (Lessons 5, 12)

supporting reasons reasons that a writer gives to support his or her opinion in an opinion piece (Lesson 12)

synonyms words that have the same or similar meanings (Lesson 7)

technical texts informative texts that explain events, procedures, ideas, or concepts; texts that often explain what happens, why something happens, how to do something, or how something works (Lesson 6)

theme the message or truth about life that a story suggests (Lessons 1, 2, 8, 9)

third-person limited point of view text in which the narrator knows only one character's thoughts and feelings (Lesson 1)

third-person omniscient point of view text in which the narrator knows the thoughts and feelings of all the characters (Lesson 1)

third-person point of view text in which the narrator is not a character in the story and uses the pronouns *he*, *she*, and *they* (Lesson 1)

time line a graphic that shows the dates when important events happened in a certain time period (Lesson 4)

topic the subject, or main idea, of a text (Lessons 4, 5, 7, 8, 10, 12)

transitional words and phrases words and phrases that indicate shifts in thought between the sentences and paragraphs of a text (Lessons 3, 7, 11)

Acknowledgments

Picture Credits 5 Shutterstock; 25 Thinkstock; 45 Thinkstock; 47 Thinkstock; 48 Shutterstock; 69 Wikipedia; 70–71 Wikipedia; 72 Public Domain; 73 Wikipedia; 74 Wikipedia; 75 Thinkstock; 76 Wikipedia; 77 Wikipedia; 80 Shutterstock; 81 Wikipedia; 82 Wikipedia; 85 Wikipedia; 86 Thinkstock; 87 Wikipedia; 88 Thinkstock; 91 Shutterstock; 93 Shutterstock; 94 Shutterstock; 117 Shutterstock; 118 (t) Thinkstock; 118–119 (bg) Thinkstock; 119 (t) NOAA; 119 (c) Thinkstock; 119 (b) Thinkstock; 120 NOAA; 121 Thinkstock; 123 Thinkstock; 126 Thinkstock; 130–131 Thinkstock; 135 Thinkstock; 137 Thinkstock; 138 Thinkstock; 159 Thinkstock; 193 Thinkstock; 194–195 Thinkstock; 196 Shutterstock; 219 Thinkstock; 220–223 (bg) Thinkstock; 220–223 (b) Thinkstock; 220 (t) Shutterstock; 221 (b) Thinkstock; 223 Wikipedia; 226 Shutterstock; 227 Wiki Commons; 230 Thinkstock; 231 Thinkstock; 232 Shutterstock; 235 Thinkstock; 237 Thinkstock; 238 Thinkstock.

Illustrations Cover Elizabeth Rosen; 6–11 Sergio DeGiorgi; 14–22 Iva Sasheva; 27–33 Colleen Madden; 36–42 Craig Orback; 71, 83, 100, 119, 122, 128–129, 131, 177–181, 184–190, 229 Q2AMedia; 160–165, 168–174 Kristina Rodanas.